8th Air Force
Lottery

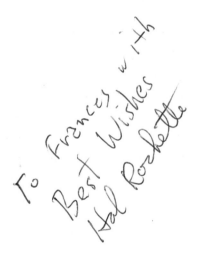

To Frances with
Best Wishes
Hal Rochette

Harold I. Rochette, 1944

8th Air Force Lottery

Winners Are Losers, Losers Are Winners

Harold I. Rochette
Lieutenant Colonel
USAFR Retired

A www.war-books.com story of courage from
Southfarm Press, *Publisher*
Middletown, Connecticut

Southfarm Press, *Publisher*

Publishing imprint of Haan Graphic Publishing Services, Ltd.
P.O. Box 1296, Middletown, Connecticut 06457
(860) 346-8798; southfar@ix.netcom.com

ISBN: 0-913337-44-7

Library of Congress Cataloging-in-Publication Data

Rochette, Harold I., 1919-
   8th Air Force lottery : winners are losers, losers are winners / Harold I. Rochette.
      p. cm.
   Includes bibliographical references and index.
   ISBN 0-913337-44-7 (pbk.)
   1. Rochette, Harold I., 1919- 2. World War, 1939-1945--Personal narratives,
American. 3. Bomber pilots--United States--Biography. 4. United States. Army Air
Forces--Biography. 5. United States. Army Air Forces. Bomber Group,384th--History. 6.
World War, 1939-1945--Regimental histories--United States. I. Title.

D790 .R644 2001
940.54'1273--dc21

                                                                      2001031357

Every effort has been made to locate the copyright holders
of all copyrighted materials and to secure the necessary permission
to reproduce them. In the event of any questions arising as to their use, the
publisher will make necessary changes in future printings.
Attention: Schools/Educational Institutions
Southfarm Press books are available at quantity discounts
with bulk purchase for educational use. For information, please write to
Special Sales Department at our address shown above.

Visit our web site at http://www.war-books.com

Cover photograph is courtesy of the Collings Foundation, Inc.,
Stow, Massachusetts
All other photographs courtesy of the author.

Contents

Chapter   **Page**

1   The Two Beginnings   9
2   Iceland and Maxwell Field   18
3   The 384th and Indoctrination   23
4   Primary, Basic, and Getting Serious   28
5   Dyersburg and My Introduction to the B-17   40
6   An Exciting Introduction to Combat   50
7   Some Relaxation and 384th Happenings   59
8   We Lose Olin Penny, Our Tail Gunner   65
9   Mission Five Is a Rough One   73
10 The Glide Bomb and Germany's Praise   78
11 Marathon Flying and Benzedrine Tablets   86
12 D-Day — the GI's Longest Day   96
13 New Tactics by Both Sides   106
14 The "Lead Banana" and Fighter Pilots   117
15 Missions Increased   123
16 Elwood Slides for Home   133
17 Bombing My Future Daughter-in-Law   138
18 The Last Mission and on to Sebring   149
19 Tampa and More Antique Veterans   160
20 Interesting Bits and Pieces   170
    "Ode to the Bombardier"   184
    Glossary   188
    About the Author   190
    Acknowledgments   194
    Further Reading   196
    Index   197

This book is dedicated
to those 43,742 brave young men
who were killed or missing in action
while battling in the skies over Europe.
May they rest in peace.

HEADQUARTERS
384TH BOMBARDMENT GROUP (H), ARMY AIR FORCES
Office of the Group Commander

APO   557
21 July, 1944

SUBJECT: Commendation.

TO   : 1st Lt. Harold I. Rochette, 544th Bombardment Squadron, 384th Bombard-
           ment Group (H), AAF.

           It gives me great pleasure to commend you upon the successful comple-
tion of your first operational tour. You have set a shining example for all
present and future combat crews of this Group to follow. Your courage, skill
and tenacity of purpose bring great credit upon yourself and to the Army Air
Forces as a whole. As you go forth into the future you leave with the knowledge of a job well done.

DALE O. SMITH,
Colonel, Air Corps,
Commanding.

Chapter One

The Two Beginnings

It was Easter Sunday morning, but not the kind of Easter Sunday morning that you would like to picture. There were no nicely dressed families going to church, no pretty little girls in their Easter finery and wide-brimmed hats.

No, this Easter Sunday was in 1944 at an air base in Labrador. Snowbanks were all around us. Snowbanks formed from snow that had been plowed from runways, ramps and taxiways. It was freezing cold and bleak outside. It was cold inside, too. We were seated in the cockpit of a B-17G Flying Fortress. I was in the copilot's seat, Lieutenant Robert James was in the pilot's seat. We were waiting for the tower to give us permission to take off. This was our Point of Aerial Embarkation (POAE) on our way to the European Theater of Operations (ETO).

We were leaving a little later than the other 14 B-17s in our group. When we taxied in yesterday afternoon, we had scraped a wing tip on one of those high snow-banks. The wing tip needed repairs, thus the delay.

Our trip had originated in Ogden, Utah, where we had picked up the B-17. With a crew of ten we flew the plane to Grenier Field, New Hampshire. We were there about four days, and I was lucky enough to hitch a ride, as copilot, to Hartford, Connecticut, where I was picked up by my family and taken to Middletown for a two-day visit. The ride from Grenier Field to Goose Bay, Labrador, had been uneventful.

Lieutenant James is a mild mannered man of about 24 or 25 years of age, soft spoken and slight of build. In civilian life he had worked for the FBI in the finger-printing department. I don't know what his job was within that department, but whatever it was, it enabled him to trap a fellow cadet who was stealing from other cadets' lockers.

In the Aviation Cadet Corps we had each taken an oath that was posted over the door to our classroom. It stated: "We will not lie, cheat or steal. Nor will we tolerate anyone who does."

The thieving cadet that Lieutenant James helped catch was drummed out of the corps, his name never to be mentioned again. What happened to him I don't know. In fact, he was in the class ahead of me, so I never actually knew him.

One cadet was drummed out of my class for cheating on a test. This drumming-out procedure consisted of forming all of the cadets in the class (hundreds of them) in ranks in front of their barracks for the announcement of the offense and the drum roll. In this case it was at 5 a.m., in a light rain, at Maxwell Field, Alabama.

This leg of our trip to the ETO was to be from Goose Bay, Labrador, to Iceland on a heading of east-northeast and would take us close to the tip of Greenland. A weather officer, who was a lieutenant colonel, the highest rank for a weather officer that I was ever to see in the Air Force, had briefed us. He was also the most wrong. He had briefed the weather as clear, ceiling and visibility unlimited (CAVU). It was anything but.

We finally got word for takeoff and we were on our way. Lieutenant James swung the plane onto the runway, I locked the tailwheel, and we took off. With the weather briefing that we'd received, we were expecting an uneventful trip. We had been told that our only concern could be German subs. German subs? We were in an airplane!

Further briefing informed us that a sub could mess up the radio beam out of the Iceland Airbase. The sub could redirect the beam. We were supposed to pick up the beam on our radio and follow it to the airfield in Iceland. Easy, no problem. But if the Germans messed it up, we might follow it out to sea and run out of gas, as sure a victory for the Germans as shooting us down.

Two fields formed the radio range, with an A being transmitted in one quadrant and an N in the other. The beam was formed as those two signals merged into a steady hum. Stay on the hum and it would lead the plane right to the runway.

It was not to be that easy. We were only a short time out when we started to get rain and wind. The further out we got, the worse it got. The wind got stronger and the rain heavier. It was a real North Atlantic storm. We were equipped with oxygen so we took the plane up to 20,000 feet to get above the storm. At that height we lost the beam, so we dropped all the way down to 150 feet. It got worse. We could see huge waves being whipped up by the wind. Big ice floes were bouncing around. I couldn't help but think that this was the ocean where the Titanic went down. I later found out that it had sunk on April 8, one week after today's date, in 1912.

We had, of course, been flying close to the beam right along. We had been getting an N signal with a background hum (the beam). So now we made corrections to get the middle of the beam — but was it the correct beam? Were we reading it right? We were 100 percent on instruments!

We had now been out of Goose Bay several hours and were really worried. We cut back on the revolutions per minute of the propellers (rpm) to 1,450 and 26 inches on the power. Air speed was now 135 miles per hour. We had no idea what our ground speed was. About then we should have been crossing over the tip of Greenland, but we couldn't use it as a checkpoint; ceiling and visibility were zero-zero.

We had a bomb bay full of 40-pound cases of K-rations. We opened the bomb-bay doors and dumped them out to lighten the aircraft. We also threw out the machine guns, ammunition, parachutes and all the radio equipment that was not being used. We broke open the parachute harness packs for their flares and compasses and threw out the harnesses.

By now everyone on board was sick. I had never been airsick and had been seasick only once, so I didn't know which one this was. I got on the intercom and called down to Dave Bronstein, our navigator, for something to heave in. Bronstein was stationed down in the nose of the plane with Gaven "Doc" Watson, our bombardier. Bronstein could find nothing but a flat piece of cardboard about a foot square. I couldn't hold the vomit, so I let it go on the cardboard and tried to balance it out of my side window. Between the wind and the bouncing, most of it landed in my lap. The mess was bad and the smell didn't help, but added to the other messes in the aircraft, it was hardly noticed.

On older model B-17s there was an opening in the top of the radio room where a machine gun was mounted. On our model G, the opening was covered with Plexiglas, as were the two waist gun positions that used to be open. Had those openings still been there, the draft would have cleared the plane. It would also have been a lot colder, since the planes furnished no heat. Our plane now smelled like a dump fire on a wind-free, 110-degree day. It can safely be said that at that time and place, our crew's feelings, both mentally and physically, were at their lowest point ever. A chaplain could have done a land-office business right there.

We informed our radio operator, Joe E. Brown (not the comedian) to send an SOS every few minutes. Due to the storm we didn't know our position so we couldn't give one. Our only hope was radar. Maybe they could pick us up on radar and give directions.

The crew members were very quiet. The usual chatter had stopped hours back. I'm sure more than a few prayers were being said. I added mine to the rest. It was the worst day I had ever experienced in my whole life to that point. Now, 55 years later, I can still say it was the worst ever. D-Day, June 6, 1944, was said to be "The

Longest Day." Well, the day of our flight to Iceland was our D-Day. In my mind, it hasn't ended yet.

By now our gas was nearly gone. We thought of cutting a couple of engines and feathering the props, but decided against it. Gas in all four tanks was about even, so there was no need to transfer between tanks.

We were still on the beam that we couldn't trust. We were desperate. We didn't know if our SOS signals were doing any good but we sent them anyway.

About then I began to wonder why I had ever wanted to be a pilot. Why had I gone through it all, just to get to sit in this seat? I wasn't seeing my life flash before my eyes, as the saying goes, but I was doing some reviewing. I'm sure James was thinking along the same lines. We were pretty quiet; there wasn't much to say.

When I volunteered for the Aviation Cadets, I had a good job in a defense plant and was earning four times the pay of a good outside job. First I had to pass a four-hour exam that required a college education, or the equivalent. With only a high school diploma, my first step was to hire a local college student to tutor me in some subjects I would need to pass. When I felt ready I went to Hartford and took the test. I passed, where some with college degrees didn't. Made me feel good.

The physical was something else. I passed everything except the eye exam. I was OK in depth perception, side vision and colorblindness. On the letters and numbers, I passed with the left eye but failed with the right. I'd been drinking carrot juice for months, until I got sick on it. It was supposed to help my vision. The sergeant told me he couldn't pass me but that there was an optometrist down the road if I wished to pursue it. I did.

The doctor asked me which eye was bad. I told him the right. He gave me a piece of cardboard to cover the left eye. They had none of the sophisticated equipment in those days that is available today. I read his chart with the bad eye. He then had me cover the right and read with the good eye. It tested bad. He found that when I covered either eye my long lashes would brush against the cardboard and cloud my vision in that eye for awhile. He gave me a note for the sergeant, who passed me without question.

By that time in the flight we could only guess as to how much gas we had left before we had to ditch. Our guess was maybe enough for another half-hour of flying. We had been on instruments for over eight hours.

A saying that I'd read back in my cadet training days kept bugging me. It was on a plaque in one of our classrooms. It kept popping into my mind. It stated, "The Air Is Even Less Forgiving Than The Sea." Now it seemed that the Air was about to disgorge us and the Sea was about to swallow us. I don't think whoever put that plaque in place ever thought it would apply so literally.

Sergeant James Shay, our engineer, was standing between and slightly behind our two seats. He was a little gray in color, sick along with the rest of us. Shay asked if we wanted our personal luggage thrown overboard with the rest of the stuff. Lieutenant James told him that it had been considered but decided against. That move would have been money out of *our* pockets. A real desperate move. Sergeant Shay survived the war and became the manager of a large department store. He was killed in a holdup.

By now it was beginning to look like we were going to get the whole nine yards. "The whole nine yards" was an expression used on fighter-plane bases in the South Pacific. A 50-caliber machine gun on one of their planes had 27 feet of ammunition in its belt. Thus, when the ammunition was all fired at one target, the target was getting the whole nine yards.

There was no question in our minds about what was to come in a ditching. In those waves we would lose the wings and sink like a rock. Even if we got out, our Mae Wests would only keep us afloat long enough to freeze to death, about 13 minutes. We kept sending out SOS signals telling of our situation. No answers.

We had about given up hope. Then, while talking to Lieutenant James, I looked past him and saw a small green light. It was on the wing of a C-47, which was about 100 feet off our left wing. The plane had British markings and had picked us up on radar. No need to say how happy we were to see it. We conversed with our signal light. Our problem was not solved yet, however. They could lead us, but they couldn't help us; only our gas tanks could do that, and their needles were bouncing on empty.

We were to experience many more tight situations on future combat missions but none quite like this one. I felt like a prisoner on death row at ten o'clock, waiting for the hour of execution at 12 o'clock. I'm sure the others felt the same way.

In less than an hour we reached the runway with a couple of engines sputtering. We were met at the ship by a sergeant with a jeep to transport us. His first words were, "Do you have any booze?" The only one on the crew who had packed any was Doc Watson, and it was only a pint. He gave it to the sergeant, and that guy and his jeep were our private transportation the whole time we were in Iceland. It wasn't until we got to the flight room that we found out that we had been battling 65 mph head winds, and our nine-hour trip had taken over 12 hours. We were also told that six of the 15 planes in our group had not made it.

Chapter Two

Iceland and Maxwell Field

Iceland was a wet, misty, barren place. At least our part of it was. There was little greenery and no trees. Everything was rock. The first thing I did was bury my flight suit under some of those rocks. The result reminded me of a pioneer's grave in the Rockies.

We were to be there only a couple of days and we had nothing to do but hang around the club and play cards or slot machines. The nearest big town was too far away, so Bob James (he had already told me that he was no relative of Jessie) and I had our private jeep and sergeant drop us off in a nearby village. The village had only two streets. They crossed to make the village center. There was a small store and a house that had one room that acted as a restaurant. There was no grass around any house. What would be a lawn back home served as a drying area for thousands of fish heads.

James and I ate at the restaurant. The meal was

served family style, chunks of pony meat in heavy gravy with whole potatoes and a loaf of bread. After the meal we walked down to the docks of that little fishing village. There I found a length of drop line with a fishhook on it. I put a piece of dead fish on it and decided to try my luck. I had been an avid fisherman in civilian life, but this was the first time I ever caught a fish that was already cleaned. I had hooked a fish of about eight pounds that must have fallen from a fishing trawler after it had been cleaned. When our sergeant picked us up he told us to take the fish to the mess hall and someone would cook it for us. We did, and they did, so we had another meal at 9 o'clock at night.

The next day we took a walk out to the flight line to admire the plane that had held out long enough to get us through. As stated, it was a B-17 and was unpainted. My first recollection of a B-17 was when my cousin and I, at ten years of age, made models of airplanes in my father's basement. We made models, carved from soft pine, of fighter planes and the B-17. People bought them for 35 cents apiece, 75 cents for a B-17. Today those prices seem real inexpensive considering that plumbers, carpenters and mechanics are being paid $20 an hour or more. Back in those days those same tradesmen were getting considerably less than a dollar an hour. I bought my first car, a 1929 model A Ford, for $15. Used, of course, but in running condition. My next car also cost $15. Another 1929 model A Ford, but it was a roadster with a rumble seat. Oh, for the good old days.

I had no idea that I would ever fly any airplane, let alone a B-17 Flying Fortress. As a matter of fact, the models were the last contact that I had with any airplane until

I joined the Army Air Force in August of 1942.

The government didn't call me until March 1943. In the meantime, I held my job at Pratt & Whitney. The money was exceptionally good, and we had every eighth day off. My shift was from midnight until seven in the morning. Seven hours, although we were paid for eight. It was ideal for me, since I liked to hunt and fish. My wife worked days, at a highly regarded insurance company, while I slept. Her wages were $31.60 for a 43-hour week. We spent our night off at a local nightclub where we knew the owners. It was called the Rose Garden, after the owner's wife.

I left by train from Meriden, Connecticut, on a snowy Tuesday morning for Fort Devens, Massachusetts. At Fort Devens, they put us in uniform and put us on another train for Nashville, Tennessee. It was a long train ride because there were a lot of long waits on sidings. We were not allowed off of the train. We slept on the seats and curled around the overhead baggage racks. Our food came from a makeshift kitchen set up in a boxcar.

At Nashville we went to a classification center. We took tests to determine which of us would be pilots, navigators or bombardiers. Most of us classified as pilots. That was because they wanted as many as possible to go to pilot training where a lot would be washed out. Some would be killed. Those who were washed out would then be re-classified as navigators, bombardiers or gunners and given another chance. I was classified as a pilot.

We were glad to leave Nashville. It was damp and misty most of the time there. All of us were coughing and had sore throats from the coal smoke in the air. Nashville-itis, it was called. Our next stop was Maxwell Field in Montgomery, Alabama. It was a pre-flight school, where we were put in good physical condition and taught to march. But the main purpose of the school was to condition our minds and to teach us meteorology, navigation, the two types of Morse code and theory of flight. There were also other subjects helpful to pilots.

During the first half, as underclassmen at Maxwell, we were called zombies and were treated by upperclassmen as if we had no minds of our own. Eating square meals (bringing each forkful to your mouth in a rectangular lift and returning the fork to the plate by the same route) was required at every meal. We called each upperclassman Mister and popped to rigid attention each time we were spoken to. The school was run like West Point by West Point graduates. There was an obstacle course called Cadet Killer and a Burma Road that was about 7 miles of rough country, brooks and obstacles. You could drop out of the run, but only on your face. It was all for a purpose. The army had made actual tabulations of the muscular movements required to pilot a plane. Those exercises, along with calisthenics, were designed to produce the body-building program required. Along with the studies, they would develop the coordination of mind and muscle that was essential for pilots.

In addition to studying the subjects previously mentioned, we also had to get passing grades in maps and charts, computers, gas and chemical warfare, physics, War Department publications and military customs and courtesies. All of that brain conditioning forced me to ask for the extra hour of lights for study each night.

It was at Maxwell Field that my wife Doris first came to visit me. We had been going together in high school and were married in August of 1941. When she arrived at Maxwell and I saw her side view, I said, "You could be pregnant." She didn't believe it, but she delivered our son Buddy in September of that year, 1943.

For the time that Doris visited me in Montgomery she stayed at the Whitley Hotel. The room rate was $3.50 a night and 25 cents for the radio. The charge for ten days was $46.50 for the best hotel in town.

When we left Maxwell we were in excellent condition and could do all the things that we were trained to do, and do them well. More on our training later in this book.

Doris and Harold Rochette at Billie Rose's Diamond Horseshoe in New York City, just before he left for Aviation Cadet Training. Rum and Coca-Cola was the popular mixed drink at that time.

Chapter Three

The 384th and Indoctrination

We took off from Iceland on April 11, 1944, headed for Stornway, Scotland. The distance was about half of what it was from Goose Bay to Iceland. We passed over a number of small islands and landed at Stornway, where we stayed overnight. The next morning we pre-flighted the plane and saw that it had its 25-hour inspection. We took off on our next leg, which was to Nuttes Corner, Ireland. Some name, but that's what they called it. On that leg we passed over five convoys and eight flattops (aircraft carriers). At the Officer's Club in Nuttes Corner we drank with Englishmen and sang songs around their piano. Dave Bronstein and I played the six-pence slot machines. I hit a double jackpot. It was an under-and-over machine. When someone hit the bottom jackpot the door would close and the top jackpot would drop down ready for the next hit. A coin from my hit stuck and held the door open. When I put in the next coin, the top jackpot came right down through. I did not give it back.

We left our plane at Nuttes Corner and took a train, then a boat, to Stone, England. We saw about 200 Sunderlands (flying boats) on the river. While at Stone we visited Hanley, which was a big town. We stayed at Beaty Hall in Stone, then took off by train for Bovington, England, and a week in combat school.

That was our last school before combat. It was different from Maxwell. There were no upper- or lower-classmen, no "square" meals. The school wasn't patterned after West Point as the cadet school had been. After the week at combat school we left for Kettering, England, and the 384th Bomb Group. Actually, the Bomb Group was at Grafton-Underwood, which was smaller than a crossroads. Kettering was the closest town of any size. We arrived at the 384th on April 28, 1944.

They showed us to our barracks. Lieutenant James and I were in one room, and Doc Watson and Dave Bronstein were in another. It was a Quonset hut. The rooms were very small and we each had a cot with a straw mattress and wool blankets. The straw pillows were in the shape of Tootsie Rolls. There were no sheets. There was a small coal stove, but no coal. Good thing we were there in the spring and summer months.

Other officers were assigned to our hut, but they weren't in, so we took a walk over to the Officers' Club. The club had a bar, of course, some card tables and a large fireplace with what looked like a stoplight over it. When lit, the stoplight would tell the mission status for the next day—green meant "yes, it's on;" red meant "no, it's canceled;" and yellow meant "not yet decided."

Bronstein and Watson joined us for dinner in the

mess hall. Bronstein was a dark-haired fellow in his early 20s. He laughed a lot, was very friendly, and nice to be around. He was from New York, where his father had a hardware store. Doc Watson was about 6 feet tall and kind of strung out. His speech was slow, with a Texas drawl. He came from a town near the Mexican border. He spoke so slowly that a person was almost tempted to help him push the words out. He was also the slowest eater I had ever seen.

The meal we had that night was one that we were to see many times. Pork chops and Brussels sprouts. In England they raised pigs and grew the sprouts in every available spot. After the meal we checked out the Post Exchange (PX) and inspected a bomb shelter. The shelter was a large pile of dirt, overgrown with grass, with a walk-in trench and an open top. Reminded me of the trenches of World War I. When we got back to the barracks, the pilot and copilot from another crew were there. We spent several hours talking to them.

At this point I should point out that a pilot and copilot received the same training and that their positions had nothing to do with their skills or abilities. The army would take one whole class of graduating cadets and send them to a B-17 transition school where they would learn everything to do with the plane they were to fly. When they graduated, the class that followed their class would be graduating Advanced Flying School and would be assigned as copilots on their crews. The pilots would then check out the copilots on the B-17.

We learned a lot about base procedures from those two officers. They told us that all of England seemed to be owned by nobility, and the Duke of Buccleuch owned the property that our base was on and several of the small towns close by. They also told us that we would need bikes to get around, but there was no need to buy them. Just wait until a crew got shot down and there would be ten available. We also learned that they, and the other two officers on their crew, were the only other occupants of our hut. All the other crews had been shot down. As fate would have it, those two men got shot down the next day and we obtained their bikes. Some system! We were then the only occupants of the barracks, and we had yet to fly a mission.

We were assigned to the 544th Squadron and its Commanding Officer (CO) was Lieutenant Colonel Nuttall. He was a regular guy, as were all the officers in charge there. The Base CO was Colonel Dale O. Smith, a West Point graduate, and there was a lot of him. He was 6 feet, 7 inches tall. We were told that when he flew a mission, they removed his seat and he sat on the floor.

As important as the war was to us, it was hard to visualize how small our part in the mammoth war would be. A war involving almost two billion people, 110 million of whom would be mobilized for military service. Hundreds of thousands of Americans would die. World War I was called the Great War, and it was, until now. It had 237 air servicemen killed in action. It had large air armadas. In the St. Mihiel offensive, 1,481 planes participated.

One would think that air combat, being as primitive as it was in World War I, would produce the first U.S. airman shot down by enemy action. This was not so.

You have to go back to July of 1898 when Sergeant Ivy Baldwin's observation balloon was brought down by

Spanish gunfire over Cuba in the Spanish-American War. He lived.

Back in our war, the 384th had been flying missions from June of 1943. They had been taking a terrible beating. They lost 100 men in the first four days. Another day a whole squadron went down in flames. Five more crews were lost on the first Schweinfurt raid, 50 men of 600 in all. In four months the 384th lost more men in combat than it had had to start with. It didn't look good, and we weren't happy to be there.

Chapter Four

Primary, Basic, and Getting Serious

Thinking back from the 384th at Grafton-Underwood, it seemed like a lot more than ten months since I entered my first flying school at Camden, South Carolina. Camden was a small town by our standards, but it was bigger than the small towns in England that I later became familiar with. The Southern Aviation School was built over a public golf course. The clubhouse was our mess hall, and a classroom and barracks were added to complete the airfield. Half of our class spent the mornings in the classroom while the other half was out learning to fly. In the afternoons, we changed positions. My flying instructor was a fellow named Joe Smollen. He was quiet and talked with a slow drawl. Must have weighed about 125 pounds soaking wet. We flew PT-17 Steermans. They were biplanes (two wings) and had a very narrow landing gear. This subjected them to ground loops, where one wing drops down to the ground and

28

the plane loops around it. Many a pilot washed out, or failed, because he couldn't master this trait.

For teaching the basics my instructor was a whiz. He taught us how to get the feel of the plane. He taught us the stall and spin characteristics and how to recover from them. After that he showed us the loops, lazy eights, pylon eights, the falling leaf, and rollovers, and coached us until we perfected each one. He taught us how to pick a field and make an emergency landing. This seems like a simple thing to do, but there was one fellow in our class who failed that operation every time he was tested. He was on his way to a washout until on his last solo flight he had real engine trouble and he had to either set down or bail out. He set it down in a spot so small, between the trees at each end, that the instructor couldn't fly it out. They took the plane out on a trailer and the man passed the test without another trial.

Back in Pre-Flight School at Maxwell Field, I had started to draw cartoons on the envelopes of the letters that I sent home to my wife. We had an excellent cartoonist in our class by the name of Jaffe. He was from the Bronx in New York and had a very creative mind and an excellent talent for drawing. I patterned my cartoons after his style. The cartoons on the envelopes continued on my letters until I graduated. Most depicted events having to do with various phases of our training. However, the first showed a zoot-suited character as he entered the cadets being transformed into a polished soldier. Another showed an out-of-character Camden pin-up girl. The local post-mistress added, "They aren't really this bad." Others had to do with cadet events—dropping cranks on the farmers' cows, crash landings, airsickness, snaprolls.

Now that I think back, what deserved a cartoon more than anything else were the gnats. All day long the gnats buzzed around our heads. They got in our eyes, ears, nose and mouth. We were continually swatting and brushing them away. Even when flying a mile up in the air, we were brushing away imaginary gnats.

But in spite of the gnats, that was the most enjoyable part of the whole cadet program. I loved to solo and fly around the clouds, shoot landings at auxiliary fields and do aerobatics.

At Camden there were auxiliary fields for us to use while flying solo, to practice landings and takeoffs. One of my fellow students was using a field near one of these as an airline terminal. He had met a girl in town who lived on a farm near one of these fields. They made a date and he landed on her farm and took her up for a ride. It wasn't long before her friends were in line for a joy ride. It lasted until he was found out and bounced.

We had a small newspaper called the Camden Kadet that called the Japanese yellow-skinned rats. Try to do that today! Today the Japanese are rewriting history. Apparently, there is no mention of the Bataan Death March, where American soldiers, prisoners of war, died at the rate of 150-200 a day. Twenty-seven percent died on the 100-mile march. The Japanese don't tell about their prison camps where prisoners had fingers chopped off to get rings. Where one water spigot furnished water for 15,000 prisoners and Americans were killed because they had a tattoo. Japanese soldiers were taught that they were superior to white people. Prisoners were treated worse than animals. Of 16,000 that worked on a bridge, 12,000 died.

In an edition of *8ᵗʰ Air Force News* it was pointed out that in Europe 95,532 Americans were taken prisoner. Of that number, 1,124 (1.2percent) died in captivity. In the Pacific, 34,648 were taken prisoner by the Japanese, 12,935 (37percent) died. A lot depended on the nationality of the captor. What a terrible price to have to pay for freedom, a freedom that students two and three generations later would take for granted, never knowing that price. A university professor recently told me that some students in his class didn't know who Hitler was, nor did they know who our enemies were in World War II.

It was at Camden that I had trouble with a tooth. I went to a local dentist. His office was on the second floor of what I believe was the highest building in town, two floors. His office was a long narrow room, much like a hallway, along the street side of the building. There were windows all along the wall and radiators under the window with a wooden top over them. The dentist's chair was right in the windowed corner of the building over Main Street. The dentist chewed tobacco and spit out the window. An awning, building long, stretched over the sidewalk under his window. It was striped green and white, only under his window it was brown. A pedal on the floor that he pumped activated his drill. I was tempted to run, but between the chewing, the spitting and the pumping, he got the job done.

From Camden, South Carolina, it was a relatively short trip to Shaw Field, which was at Sumpter. However, as short as it was, they sent us by train. The distance was short, but with layovers the time was long. At Shaw Field I met the first of my two flight instructors. His name escapes me, but I remember that he was about six feet tall and of average weight. He was from the Bronx, New York, and you knew it when he spoke.

For some reason he didn't like me. It couldn't have been my flying because he gave me good marks. I was assigned another instructor named Robert Prince, and he was a prince of a guy. He was about 19 or 20, newly married, and lived in town. Lieutenant Prince was a crackerjack pilot and an excellent instructor. Guess that's why he had that job at so young an age.

We flew the BT-13 Vultee Vibrator at Shaw Field. It was a monoplane, a single-wing plane with that wing on the bottom. Its engine was a Pratt & Whitney and was much more powerful than the one on the Steerman back at Camden. It is a heavier and faster plane too.

We had a day off before schooling began, so a friend and I took a bus into town. Sumpter was the closest town to a large army base, so the town was full of soldiers. Walking down the street we were being saluted by every soldier we passed. We didn't understand why, so we asked the first officer we met. He explained that the gold emblem on our hats, a pair of gold wings with a vertical propeller in the center, was the cause. "The men are in boot camp and taught to salute all officers and any rank they don't recognize." That was the one and only time we went into that town.

The school at Camden was called a Primary Training School, while the school at Shaw Field was called a Basic Training School. The other two schools in the Cadet Training Program were Pre-Flight, which I finished at Maxwell Field, and the Advanced, which followed Basic.

At Shaw Field we bought a haircut coupon that

was good for three haircuts. It cost $1.05. I also had to get a certificate to buy a pair of shoes.

Two notable firsts happened in Basic School. One was my first flying crisis and the other was the birth of our son Harold Rochette Jr. on September 27, 1943. As his date of birth drew near, I was nervous and jumpy. I couldn't go home to be with Doris, so all I could do was wait. Lieutenant Prince and his young wife tried to console me by keeping me occupied in the evenings. I got to know them pretty well and we became real friends.

After we students soloed the BT-13, we had our first cross-country flights. We were given a map with the route of the flight marked out. All we had to do was follow it from point to point. Simple as that seems, some of us got lost at times. When that happened we would drop down on a small hamlet and read the sign on the railroad station, find it on the map, and in some cases, follow the railroad to the next checkpoint. We also started night flying in that school. That's where I met my first crisis.

In night flying the instructor took the student up to a quadrant and held in that spot until the tower called them in for a landing. You then came down and got into the landing pattern, a rectangular pattern around the field, a few hundred feet up with the downwind leg running 180 degrees from your landing direction. The base leg was a 90-degree turn from there, and the approach another 90-degree turn to line up with the runway.

We were called in for the first landing and Lieutenant Prince made it. We went up again. This time I made the landing. Prince left the plane and sent me up alone. I found the quadrant and held until called in. I entered the downwind leg and continued the pattern into the approach. Properly aligned, and halfway down the approach, the windshield suddenly turned black. The engine, which was directly in front of me, had an oil line break. Seeing the runway lights through the windshield was next to impossible. I pulled down my goggles, threw back the canopy, and half standing up, leaned out to my left as far as I could while still controlling the plane.

It happened so fast, and so close to the ground, that I had no time to use the radio. The people on the ground didn't realize what was going on. With my goggles down, and my head out of the cockpit, I could see for a brief moment and make corrections, but the oil again quickly took over and covered my goggles. I threw off the goggles, and with my left hand palm forward in front of my eyes, I squinted between two fingers. The wind and oil were tough. The plane hit hard, but as soon as I was on the ground, I dropped back into the cockpit and brought the plane to a stop. I was off the landing strip, but safe. I could easily have been added to those cadets already killed in this class.

As could be expected, both the casualty rate and the washout rate were lower in Basic than they were in Primary. When we graduated from Advanced School we were told that due to washouts, flying accidents and failure to pass tests, only one person in 40 taking the entrance exam would receive pilot wings.

BEFORE

AFTER

A/C ROCHETTE, H. I.

Harold Rochette at Primary Training at Camden, South Carolina. The art work, by the author, is taken from envelopes of his letters sent home.

Like many kids, Harold Rochette doodled his way through school. He learned to draw cartoons in high-school art class. During pilot training, finding himself in school again, Rochette spent time drawing cartoon doodles on the envelopes of the letters he sent home to his wife.

FROM THIS

TO THIS

TO THIS

During training, the author flew each of these planes, top to bottom: Steerman PT-17, flown during Primary Training at Camden, South Carolina; BT-13 Vultee Vibrator, flown while in Basic School at Shaw Field, South Carolina; AT-10, flown in Advanced Training at George Field, Illinois. The art work is from the envelopes the author sent home to his wife.

TO THIS, THE B-17 FLYING FORTRESS

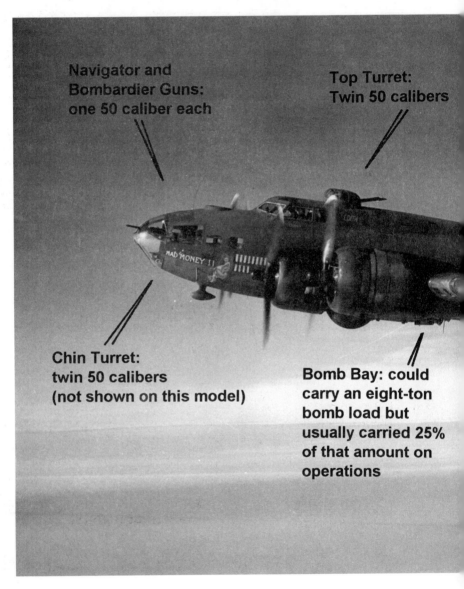

Navigator and Bombardier Guns: one 50 caliber each

Top Turret: Twin 50 calibers

Chin Turret: twin 50 calibers (not shown on this model)

Bomb Bay: could carry an eight-ton bomb load but usually carried 25% of that amount on operations

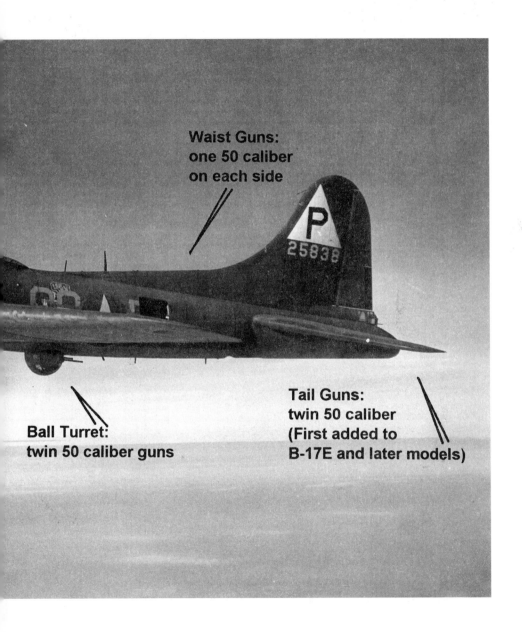

Waist Guns:
one 50 caliber
on each side

Ball Turret:
twin 50 caliber guns

Tail Guns:
twin 50 caliber
(First added to
B-17E and later models)

Chapter Five

Dyersburg and
My Introduction
to the B-17

When we finished Basic School at Shaw Field we took another train ride, to a colder climate this time, George Field, Illinois. There we flew the twin-engine AT-10. We flew formation for the first time and had two engines to worry about.

We had a problem with frost in the mornings. I mean heavy frost, the kind that had to be scraped from the wings and fuselage with the heavy plastic container that housed the airplane checklist. The frost was present every morning and was a result of the moist air being supplied by the Great Lakes.

Although we never used it again, we did night formation flying here. In the ready-room we wore goggles with red lenses. That helped our night vision while flying. We took them off when we went outside into the dark. After George Field, we received our wings and were commissioned second lieutenants or flight officers.

Cadets who were flight officers had a different bar than the gold bar of second lieutenants. It was blue. It always seemed unfair to me that a cadet became a flight officer, suggesting some sort of inferiority, when he had passed all the trials and tests the rest of the class passed.

Graduation day was December 5. We had thought that it might be delayed to coincide with Pearl Harbor Day, but I guess they needed crews in the ETO too badly to waste two days, so we graduated on schedule. By far, most of us were commissioned second lieutenants. I received my gold bars and my silver wings. I had to pin them on myself because none of my family members were present. After wings were pinned on, the custom was to give a dollar to the first person who saluted you. I gave my dollar to a staff sergeant. I suspect that a lot of enlisted people just cruised around the base that day, maybe even collected an extra day's pay.

Two days after graduation I was home and saw our son for the first time. If I must say so, he was a good-looking kid. My family and I had about a week together before I had to report to the next base. I hadn't been home in nine months. I spent a good portion of it visiting friends that I had worked with and some that I had played football and basketball with. My father enjoyed taking me around to see his friends and family. He was proud of the uniform, and especially proud of the silver wings. There were a lot of uniforms around, but not many pilot's wings. He even took me to a floating crap game, a place where I shouldn't have been, but where he had friends. The stay at home was all too short. We took a lot of pictures, then I was off to my next training school, Phase Training at Dyersburg, Tennessee.

I could now have my wife and son with me, so my first job at Dyersburg was to find a place for us to live. I found a room in a private home. It was small and had a small stove. I sent for Doris and Harold Jr. (Buddy, nicknamed by my father) and we moved in. We moved out as fast as we had moved in. There was no way I could get that stove to operate, it was too small and the soft coal too large. It was too cold for the baby.

We moved to a room in the Cordell Hull Hotel. Buddy slept on a pillow in a bureau drawer. The next day we called home. My mother agreed to keep Buddy, so Doris took him home, then she came back down. This time we found a room in a better house, in a better neighborhood. The house was owned by a Mrs. Conn. I called her Mrs. Connecticut after my home state. Her only rules were no drinking, no wild parties, no children.

Mrs. Conn had a cat named Snowball. It may have looked like a snowball when it was born, but it had turned a solid light gray, due to the soft-coal smoke and dust in the air all the time. I purchased a small cloth mouse for Snowball to play with. She got real interested when I sprinkled a few drops of sardine oil on it. She eventually got tired of the hoax and sat there looking at me until I gave her one of the sardines that she knew I had in the refrigerator. Doris and I took no meals at Mrs. Conn's house. We usually had breakfast at a little restaurant a short distance away. It looked like a hot-dog stand that was enclosed. Inside was a three-sided counter with stools. The cook worked at a grill against the back wall and inside the counters. The meals were varied but they all came with pinto beans, even when it was requested that they be left off.

I ate lunch at the base, but Doris and I always had dinner together, most of the time at a restaurant in the Cordell Hull Hotel. It was at that hotel that I was cited for my only infraction committed while in service. One evening it was hotter than a witch's teat, so I took off my jacket. An MP saw me and gave me the infraction. Luckily, I didn't have to serve any time.

While at Dyersburg, Bob James and his sweetheart Evelyn were married. One of his classmates, Bob Johnson, was his best man. Evelyn was a pretty girl from Virginia, quiet and easy to get along with. A wedding picture was taken on the church steps. In that picture were six men, all pilots. All were killed in combat except James and me. He and I were almost always on the same plane.

At Dyersburg, I got my first look at a real B-17 Flying Fortress. By today's standards it wasn't very big, but at the time it was huge. The B-17G was 79 feet, 9 inches long, with a wingspan of 103 feet, 9 inches. It was 10 feet, 1 inch high. It's wing area was 1,420 square feet. That gave it its stability and ability to still fly when heavily damaged. It had four 1,200-hp Wright Cyclone, turbocharged radial piston engines, top speed was 290 mph and top ceiling was 35,600 feet. (We never flew above 30,000 feet.) Its range was 2,000 miles with a 5,000-pound bomb load, increased to 17,600 pounds over shorter distances. It had 12 50-caliber machine guns. Its long dorsal fin earned it the affectionate name "the big-assed bird."

There were 12,731 B-17s built, and the first American combat loss of World War II was a B-17 shot down by Japanese zeroes. It was on its way to Pearl Harbor.

Our first flights on oxygen were made at Dyersburg while practice bombing at 20,000 feet. We did have, however, some previous experience with oxygen, or rather, the lack of it. To show us the effects of the lack of oxygen on our minds and bodies, the Army Air Force had put us in a large, heavily built metal cylinder, much like an above-ground service station gas tank with windows. We were put inside in groups of eight and told to write our names over and over on a sheet of paper. As our breathing used up the oxygen, our name writing became wavy. It became more and more wavy as the oxygen disappeared until it was almost a straight line. We thought we were still writing our name in a legible manner. Oxygen was then pumped into the tank. As we received more and more oxygen, our name writing became more and more clear until it returned to normal. That demonstration was meant to show us how easy it would be to die from lack of oxygen and not even realize it. It was effortless and painless. I often wondered why the states didn't use that method to execute criminals.

Years later I read of a dancing girl who died from lack of oxygen at a stag party. She was to spring from a large cardboard cake to perform her dance. When she did not, it was found that she had smothered in the tight enclosure. She had died, unaware, with a smile on her face.

Training at Dyersburg was fun. We had a chance to bring the B-17 down to fence height while giving the gunners practice on ground targets. It was done on a deserted island in the Mississippi River. We did some night bombing at high altitude while on oxygen. We never actually used either of those activities in combat.

There was one humorous happening that took place on a night practice bombing mission. The center of Dyersburg was a square, and the streets around it were laid out in a pattern so that, when lit up at night, it resembled the bombardiers' target. They were using 100-pound sand bombs with flash powder in their noses. One bombardier mistook the town for the target. After the first run, the town's sheriff realized the error and got on the phone to the base. He was excited as he explained the error, and before dropping the phone hollered, "They're coming over again, I'll be back!" as he headed for the cellar.

One part of the school that was not fun was when they put a damaged B-17 on the ramp with a floodlight on it. Lieutenant James and I had done the damage. On the base they had some B-17Es that had oil-operated superchargers. The difference between this model, and the one with the electric superchargers, was that they needed considerable warming up of the oil before takeoff, or the engines could run away. Neither James nor I had ever made the acquaintance of the oil-operated type, so we took off without the proper warm-up.

We were barely airborne when all four engines ran wild. There was a terrible racket and much vibration. A cylinder head and oil line on number one broke. Number two started to smoke and a cylinder head on number three broke. The engine caught on fire. All that happened about 20 feet in the air and at about 120 mph. We had pulled 100 inches on all engines. James immediately set the plane down, and we came to a braking stop using every inch of the runway. That was something that was not done very often, taking off and landing a B-17 on a 5,000-foot runway in less than a minute. It usually took the whole runway to do either. When they put the flood-lighted plane on the ramp, they also put a sign in front of it stating how much it would cost to repair and the number of man-hours it would take. The cost to the government was $39,456 and 600 man-hours. James and I were happy they didn't include our names.

While at Dyersburg we found it hard to get whiskey of any kind, plenty of rum, but no whiskey. I wrote to my father of this and he sent down a case of bourbon. It was labeled "Dishes—handle with care." It was intended that we would drink the bourbon at the club on the base, which we were doing until Mrs. Conn told us we could have a drink at home. From that point on her rules on drinking and partying went down the drain. She and Bob Johnson were our best customers, and almost constant companions.

There were many accidents at the base. Planes crashed and crews bailed out. Bob Johnson's crew was one that had to bail out, engine trouble at night. Johnson's copilot, a burley redhead named Rogers, had been a Miami policeman in civilian life. He bailed out in good fashion, but in the dark he landed in a pigpen. Scared the hell out of a lot of porkers and hurt his back so bad he had to be discharged from the service.

Doris and I were able to visit Memphis, with Bob and Evelyn James. It was nice to have the quiet and solitude of a hotel room for a change. It might be worth mentioning that one officer, in training at this base, had all the comforts of home. He had his wife, child, maid and chauffeur-driven car with him. We were told that he was from Texas and owned a bunch of oil wells.

On February 28, 1944, we were flying over Memphis at 17,000 feet on oxygen. There was a ceiling (height of clouds above earth) at 1,200 feet and visibility of one and a half miles. We were climbing, in formation, when our number four engine started to smoke and shoot oil. We feathered (turned the propeller blades into the wind) the prop, but at 200 rpm the feathering pump burned out and it windmilled and unfeathered itself. We couldn't see the ground at all, so we came down through the overcast on instruments. We were about 70 miles from the base at about 1,000 feet. Had to grope around in the soup on three engines, plus one that was windmilling. Barely cleared a radio tower with our right wing. We did land safely, but we agreed that it was no fun flying on instruments with three engines. Never a dull moment.

There were no eventful happenings of note until March 9, 1944. Just about a year since I had left home. On that date we were flying a cross-country that took us into the Great Lakes region. There was a solid overcast (undercast to us) at the Lakes, but otherwise CAVU. We were at 20,000 feet on oxygen, blown off course, low on gas, and lost. We were about ready to tell the crew to bail out when we picked up the beam from Chanute Field. We followed it in and landed in the dark.

We filled the tanks with 1,558 gallons of gas and took off again. We were only out a short distance when we had engine trouble on number two and had to return to Chanute. We spent the night. The next morning, on takeoff, we discovered that we had a vibrating right wheel. We left the wheels in the down position and flew the three hours back to Dyersburg. At Dyersburg we had the pattern cleared for an emergency landing. Turned out that the wheel was out of line. I hoped that the planes in the ETO received better maintenance than those old models. We had made three emergency landings on one trip and had burned over 2,000 gallons of fuel. With all that excitement, who needed combat?

Before we left Dyersburg, we all got together for a party at the Officers' Club. Everything went well until the party was breaking up. At that time Bob Johnson and his wife Nell had a spat. It wasn't much at that time but after they got home it really turned ugly. Nell was a tall southerner, very independent and easily provoked.

The next morning we left for Ogden, Utah, where we picked up the plane that flew us overseas. All of our wives left for their homes. Johnson and Nell hadn't made up and were still mad at each other. We spent only one day at Ogden, and then we were off to Grenier Field, New Hampshire. I made my visit home from there, then it was off to Goose Bay, Labrador, and overseas.

GEORGE FIELD

LAWRENCEVILLE, ILLINOIS

The subjects of Harold Rochette's cartoons on the envelopes he sent home to his wife during flight training included snap rolls, air pockets, and landing a plane on a cow!

Chapter Six

An Exciting Introduction to Combat

There was not a long history of the 8th Air Force but there was a lot of history for so short a period. The 8th was activated on January 28th, 1942, with 74 officers and 81 enlisted men. Brigadier General Asa N. Duncan was in command. The 8th furnished the B-25s and crews for the attack on Tokyo that was led by Lieutenant Colonel Jimmy Doolittle in April of 1942.

Putting the American Air Force together in England was a piecemeal operation. Headquarters was established in a closed girls' boarding school, only a few miles from the Royal Air Force (RAF) Headquarters. By that time both Germany and England had already given up daylight bombing due to unacceptable heavy losses. The British tried, with no success, to convince American leaders to give up their commitment to high-altitude, daytime, precision bombing. They thought that the B-17s and B-24s were better suited to other tasks.

The first mission for the 8th was assigned to the 384th Bomb Group at Grafton-Underwood, our base. Twelve B-17s bombed railway yards at Rouen on August 17, 1942. All 12 returned safely.

Planes and combat crews were hard to attain. It wasn't until April 17, 1943, that 100 planes could be put up at the same time. The military took a long time building the Air Force. But build it they did. Eventually the 8th was to be the most powerful force ever assembled and would have its own museum in Savannah, Georgia.

As bombers and crews arrived they flew missions escorted by RAF Spitfires. The Spitfire's range was only 175 miles, the same as the P-47s that came from America. With modifications that range was increased to 230 miles. With the addition of 150-gallon belly tanks the range was again increased, to 425 miles.

It was the practice of the 8th Air Force to use each pilot as copilot on his first mission. He would fly with an experienced crew for the break-in flight. On May 7, 1944, Bob Johnson was the first of our Dyersburg group to fly. He flew as copilot with an experienced crew, as was the custom. Five of that crew were flying their last mission. They would then be sent back to the States. The mission was a milk run, a short mission with little fighter opposition or flak expected.

They were no sooner in flak (bursts of shells from batteries of large guns on the ground) range when they received a direct hit in front of the waist door escape hatch. The hit blew the ship in half. It exploded, and only two parachutes were seen. No chance that Johnson had made it. It takes a lot longer for the pilots to get out, and on a direct hit they never could have made it.

When we got the news, both Lieutenant James and I had the same thought. How would Nell take it, after the argument they had on their last night together?

As stated, that was supposed to be a milk run and it was the only ship lost from the base. There were two planes lost on the mission before that, five of 18 before that, and a whole formation of nine before that.

We were about to fly our first mission in that phase of the war that was aimed at German aircraft assembly plants, ball-bearing factories, and enemy fighters, both in the air and on the ground.

On Friday the 13th of May, we flew our first mission. No time to be superstitious. We didn't know where we were going until we got to the briefing room. An orderly woke us up about 1:30 in the morning. We went to the latrine, cleaned up and shaved. We had to shave our beards before every mission if we were to wear an oxygen mask, both for comfort and for a good fit.

Our next stop was breakfast. Before a mission, fliers could have eggs any way they wanted them. Not powdered but real eggs, and only for the flyers. For some it would be their last meal.

The mess hall was cafeteria style and you helped yourself, until you got to the man who was cooking the eggs. Some cafeterias have metal trays with compartments for each different helping of food, and you don't use dishes. This cafeteria used trays with no compartments, and you put your food on dishes and the dishes on the tray. Doc Watson was so flustered and preoccupied that he went down the line putting the food directly on his tray as though it had compartments. It wasn't until he reached the fellow cooking the eggs that he realized what he was doing. He went back and started over again.

After breakfast we went to briefing. The mission's route was plotted on a big map on the wall at the front of the room. When the briefing officer uncovered the map, a big groan went out from the gathering. It was just about as long a mission as could be flown, over 2,000 miles round trip to Setten, Germany. We were getting the whole nine yards on our first mission. We were shown on the map where we could expect the heaviest flak and fighter attacks.

The target was a Focke-Wulf aircraft plant, and cloud coverage at the target was 80 percent. We had a 500-foot ceiling over England. That meant a dangerous crawl through clouds with 5,000 pounds of bombs and 2,700 gallons of gasoline, over a 10-ton load.

Lieutenant James and I left the briefing and went over to pick up our parachutes, oxygen masks and escape kits. In addition, we were given a small, heavily waxed cardboard box of candy, about 2 by 3 by 4 inches. It contained fudge, some striped peppermint candy, and some gum in the form of Chiclets. That was our subsistence ration for the whole trip.

The escape kit, which we would open only if we were shot down, contained a map of the territory that we would fly over, an escape compass, and some money of the country whose air space we would violate.

We hopped into a jeep and were driven out to the ramp where our plane was parked. It was the plane that Lieutenant James and I would fly on almost all of our missions. It was shiny and new, a B-17G, just like the one we had left in Ireland.

We walked around the outside of the plane, checking the wheels, ailerons, supercharger, wheel spokes, and kicking the tires. We introduced ourselves to the crew chief and asked if there was anything we should know, anything peculiar to the aircraft. He said no, so we climbed aboard.

I entered through the front hatch, which is right under the pilot's seat and in front of the number two engine. James entered right behind me. We had pushed our parachutes in before we grasped the edge of the hatch and swung up. The parachutes that we carried were the chest type. This means that they are round, about 10 inches in diameter, and about 18 inches long. They have two heavy clips on the back that attached to rings on the body harness that we were wearing. We wore the body harness all the time, along with our Mae West, but only attached the parachute if we were bailing out of the plane.

The Mae West was an inflatable vest worn under the parachute harness. It was named after a movie star of that era who was rather buxom. If it were to be named today it would probably be called a Dolly Parton.

We strapped ourselves in our seats, and I read the checklist to James as he performed the motions. As we awaited the signal to start engines I checked out the crew on the intercom.

The word came to start engines. Eighty 1,200 hp engines can make an awful racket on a quiet morning. It was daylight as we taxied the plane along the paved strip to the runway. As we taxied along we wove from side to side so as to get a clear view ahead. The plane in front of us was rolling down the runway. We swung around onto the runway and waited about 30 seconds. I locked the tailwheel and we started down the left side of the runway, so as to avoid the propwash of the plane in front of us that had used the right side. James was pushing the throttles to get maximum power, but the ship was not responding as it should. Our flight engineer was standing between our seats and checking the instruments.

As we reached the halfway point on the runway, we were only doing 80 mph, too slow. I again checked each of the controls in order; they had been checked just before the takeoff roll. When I got to the turbo-supercharger dial I found it to be only on the number four position. I dialed it to full power, raised the stop barrier and dialed it into the emergency position.

All four engines raced and the ship shuddered from the strain. We were picking up speed, but would we get enough in time, the end of the runway was coming up fast. We were now far past the point of no return. I had all that I could do to keep from helping James lift that bird into the air. He was as good a B-17 pilot as there was, and the second-best pilot in the Army Air Force. I knew that takeoff was his for better or for worse. But it was hard staying off of the controls and I expended more energy twisting and straining with my body English than he did flying the plane. My thoughts swung back to the trip over the North Atlantic. That was slow death, this was death much faster. We reached the end of the runway with our wheels still on the pavement and the little town of Geddington right in front of us. I swear that our wheels were still on the ground as we left the runway. We were half flying, half rolling, as both of us tried to lift us into the air. We cleared the town beneath us, but I bet we broke a lot of dishes with the vibration. We climbed slowly, and as we got up to the proper speed, I gradually dialed back on the turbos.

Forty years later, when we visited Bob and Evelyn at their home in Virginia, Bob asked, "Remember that time when you saved our bacon?" I didn't know if he was referring to that mission or a future mission, and I didn't ask.

We climbed into that 500-foot ceiling and picked up our buncher beacon on the radio. Many planes were lost, and more would be, as the result of collisions in that type of overcast. Too many planes in too little space, and it always seemed to be cloudy over England. They got about 14 days of rain a month at this time of the year.

Our squadron assembled at the beacon and set out for the next assembly point where we formed as a group and took off for the target. We slowly climbed to altitude as we headed for the English Channel.

From our base, located 60 miles in from the channel, we flew a straight course while over England and the water. We didn't fly a beeline to the target. We didn't want the enemy to know what the target was until we got there. We also had to avoid the known flak batteries, so we flew a sort of zigzag course, namely evasive action. We weren't long over enemy occupied territory when we saw our first flak. It came up in bursts of four. It had our altitude figured out, but it was off to our left.

That flak was the first Lieutenant James and I had ever seen. It didn't look that dangerous. We couldn't hear it, and those black mushrooms looked harmless.

About half an hour later we saw the flak that we had heard about. We saw the group in front of us fly through it. The sky was black. Five minutes later we were

in it. Those gunners were right on the mark and several
near hits bounced our ship. It sounded like someone
pounding on a wash tub as the bursts closed in. We continued on, still unscathed, but there was more to come.
We were still hours from the target when we met our
first fighter opposition. They were Messerschmitt 109s,
and they attacked from the rear. They usually hit from
either the front or the rear. Fewer guns were shooting at
them from that angle.

There were about 20 of them and they shot down
two B-17s in back of us before they were engaged by our
"little friends" the fighters, the P-47s. As we approached
the IP (initial point) where we would make our turn onto
the bomb run, the fighters left us. They left because they
didn't want to get caught in the barrage of flak that was
to be thrown at us.

On the bomb run we had to fly straight and level.
The bombardier flew the plane with his bombsight. That,
however, took place only in the lead plane. The rest of
the bombardiers toggled out their bombs when they saw
the lead plane's flare and its bombs drop. Later on in the
war those men would be sergeants and would be called
togglers.

Usually a bomb run was about eight minutes long,
but could be 20 in a strong head wind. Flak was heavy
and made a big black cloud. Nothing to do but sit there
and take it.

We saw the lead plane's bombs drop, and our ship
lifted as Doc dropped our load. He shouted into the intercom, "Bombs away. We're working for ourselves
now." We heard that many more times in the future. We
came off the bomb run and turned toward home. The

fighters pounced on us again, but not before they gave their buddies with the 20-mm cannons their shot. The Germans had some FW-90s and BF-100s that were more heavily armored than the regular fighters, and they were equipped with 20-mm cannons. Sometimes they sat out of range of our guns and fired shells into our formation. Other times they came in, sometimes abreast, sometimes single file, and held their fire until they could not miss.

This time they stood off and peppered us. Several ships received damage. The ship to our right lost an engine. They dropped back, put out the fire, and feathered the engine. The fighters were all over the group in front of us. Our "little friends" couldn't stay with us that far in, so all the enemy had to fear were the guns on the fortresses. Sixty-seven percent of all enemy fighters that were shot down were shot down by gunners on those bombers. I saw two planes go down in front of us. One just rolled over and went into a dive with smoke pouring from it. The other went into a slow corkscrew spiral. I saw only three chutes, total, from the two ships.

We were dead-tired when we entered the de-briefing room back at the base. De-briefing was just a session of questions: Where'd you get the flak? How heavy? See any fighters? How many? Who went down? A shot of scotch was waiting for us, and coffee and sandwiches. One of our crew didn't drink, so I took his scotch, too. The box of candy was still in my pocket. I was too excited, and busy, on the mission to eat any. I learned the next day that there were always children in town waiting for crew members. The familiar "Got any gum, chum?" was their greeting. After that I always saved my candy for them. It was the only candy they ever got.

Chapter Seven

Some Relaxation and 384th Happenings

We were standing down the next day, so Bronstein and I took a bike ride into Brigstock to look it over. It was about the size of Geddington and only a short distance away. It was close to 1700 (5:00 pm) so we waited until a small shop that sold fish and chips opened. They were out of fish so we had to settle for the chips (french fries). They were take-out and wrapped in newspaper. We ate the chips, newsprint and all.

It would not be dark for several hours yet, so we hopped on the bikes and headed to Geddington. The main attraction in Geddington was the Star Pub. It sold beer until it ran out and the bar man "put up the towel." On occasion they would put up a bottle of scotch, gin or whiskey, mostly scotch though. The bottle (they never had more than one) was held in a clamp, upside down, on the back bar. It had a spigot that turned to dispense the liquor. We never bought the liquor because there was so little, and the townspeople waited for it. They would get their one small glass and nurse it the whole evening.

The British drank their beer warm, so of course we did too. When an American has his first taste, the question always came up, "Where do you keep the horse?"

We played a couple of games of skittles. Skittles is a game a little like bowling. The idea is to knock down ten pins that are formed, in a diamond shape, on a table with a net around it. You do this by throwing a hockey-like puck at them.

Forty years later my wife and I, and a friend from Grafton-Underwood, played on the same table and she beat the both of us.

Bronstein and I rode our bikes back to the barracks over the same runway that we had the close call on the day before. It was also the same runway that three GIs were riding home on a couple of months back. It was a pitch-black night and they had a strong wind blowing against their backs. Taking off on the same runway was a British Lancaster bomber. Neither the bikes nor the Lancaster had any lights on, due to the blackout regulations. Those three men rode right into those propeller blades. They told me it was a terrible mess. That was the most drastic of many bicycle accidents. I wonder how that was reported to the folks back home?

The 384th Bomb Group was made up of four squadrons, the 544th, 545th, 546th and 547th. In the first four days of combat the 384th lost 100 men, 40 of whom were from the 544th squadron. In the first three weeks the 544th suffered half of all the losses. I was beginning to wonder if we were part of a hard luck squadron.

On July 25, 1943, the 384th lost an entire squadron,

The Eleanor Cross of Geddington, in the foreground, is a popular tourist attraction in England today. During the war, however, the pilots' interest lay more in the Star Pub in the background, where they hoisted a few.

and all but one were of the 544th. Only ten aircraft of the entire group returned, and every one of them had suffered heavy battle damage. It had been a heartbreak running battle of two hours and 16 minutes.

Those men, boys most of them, were the pioneers of the 384th, and of the 8th Air Force. Their average age was 19. It took a lot of 17-year-olds to average out a 40-year-old officer. They were facing a far superior foe, a foe that had the advantage of experience, firepower and territory. They were seeing the best fighter planes in the world. Planes that the Germans had years to plan, build, experiment with and perfect. Planes like the Focke-Wulf 190s, Messerschmitt 109s, 110s and 210s. They also saw Junkers 88s and Dornier 217s. Later in the war, after we came home, the 8th would see some German jets. Luckily, too late to help the Germans. American crews, at the beginning of "our war," were few in number. Replacements filled in for planes lost, and then replacements filled in for the replacements as they went down. It was a long agonizing time before any crew was able to do the required number of missions to complete a tour.

No matter what the number of missions required to complete a tour, there was always the psychological factor in a set known number. Ernie Pyle wrote, "Flyers get to within three or four missions of finishing and get so nervous they about jump out of their skin. So many are killed on the last few missions. There should be a way to sneak up on it."

The first to finish the required number of missions was the crew of the "Memphis Belle." They were a much-celebrated group of men when they returned to the States. They were further honored by a visit of the Queen of England and other royalty. It was that rare an accomplishment. Many men had died and many planes had been shot down before that important goal had been reached by the Memphis Belle and the 8th Air Force.

Sometime in the future we may have to worry only about the loss of the planes and not the pilots. North Dakota Sate University, with the cooperation of the Massachusetts Institute of Technology, Texas A& M and the University of California at Berkeley, is working on a guidance system for airplanes that needs no pilot. Our Navy wants to send the pilotless planes into combat. This project is of course top secret. Only the people working on it know the details. Those people and possibly the Chinese.

White trails of condensed water vapor sometimes form in the wake of an aircraft. Called contrails, these white streaks are pretty to look at but are dangerous to fly through. While flying in formation on bombing runs, contrails seriously reduced pilots' visibility.

Chapter Eight

We Lose Olin Penny, Our Tail Gunner

Our second mission was to Calais, France, inside the West Wall. The report was "undercast en route and broken at the target." We were awakened at 0230 (2:30 AM) and had breakfast at 0300, briefing at 0330. After briefings, church services were available for all faiths. I attended the Catholic service. After that first mission I knew it wouldn't hurt, and we could use the help.

This day's target was a rocket installation. At the time we didn't know what they were to be used for. We called them no-ball targets. They turned out to be the launching ramps for the buzz bombs that would later plague London. We gathered our gear, mounted the plane and taxied out to takeoff, all in the proper order and on command. We went through our checklist. This time we both checked the turbo-supercharger dial.

After takeoff we had to climb through that ever-present overcast again. As the saying goes, "We held our breath." Before the war was over the 8th Air Force would lose over 300 aircraft and crews to collisions in that soup.

It is easy to understand how those losses piled up. There were 27 groups on 27 different airfields in the vicinity. Each of the 27 groups had four squadrons and each squadron six or seven aircraft, all taking off in the same short period of time. In England there were 131 airfields in a space about the size of Vermont. Nuff said. We assembled our formation according to the standard procedure and started our climb to bombing altitude, 26,500 feet. We were carrying six 1,000-pound bombs. It was a relatively short mission and we might have called it a milk run except for a tough break for our tail gunner, Olin Penny.

Sergeant Penny had been with us from the time our crew was formed at Dyersburg. He was a blond kid, about 18, and of slight build. Very polite, and intelligent. Only two days before, he had come to me, after we had finished our first mission, and asked two questions: What was the procedure for becoming an Aviation Cadet? and Would [I] recommend [him] for admission to that training? I told him the procedure and the qualifications and said, "Yes, I'd be glad to recommend you."

We saw no fighters on this mission but we did get a lot of heavy flak. We were getting holes in the ship. One gas line had been cut and some pieces of flak were bouncing around in the bomb bay among the bombs. We made two passes at the target but didn't drop the bombs.

The flak was very accurate as well as heavy. We made a wide turn when leaving the target, and four bursts of flak hit right in the spot where we would have been. Olin Penny was sitting back in the tail and received a lot of flak. Both legs were badly shot up. The temperature was 40 degrees below zero and the trip home had to have been very painful for him. To make matters even worse, we had to take extra time to go up to the Wash and dump the bombs so we could land.

The Wash is a big bay on the east coast of England. When the war ended there must have been a million tons of bombs under the water of that bay. We could have dropped the bombs if we could have seen the target, but the broken undercast that had been forecast turned to a complete undercast, and we couldn't dump the bombs blindly on the French. Later we had Pathfinder B-17s to lead the way and, with their Path Finder (PFF) equipment, find the target through the clouds.

Sergeant Penny had to forget his aspirations of becoming an Aviation Cadet. They had to take off big chunks of flesh and muscle from both legs. He was on his way home after only two missions. He was replaced by Staff Sergeant John Kew.

It was four days before our next mission, so James and I had a chance to run down to London. The first thing we saw when we got off the train was a big sign: Hollywood Milk Bar. We both wanted a strawberry milkshake and that's what we ordered. What we got was powdered milk, powdered flavoring and no ice cream. Nuff said. We ate at the Red Cross Canteen and set out to see the town. As it was getting dark, we took some rides on several two-deck buses, saw the Tower of London, the House of Commons and a plaque with the name of Mr. Crapper on it, the man who invented the you-know-what. It was pitch black by now, so we went to a hotel and went to sleep listening to buzz bombs fall on the city.

We left London the next afternoon and got back to the base in time to go down to the flight line and watch our planes return from a raid. On one of the planes was a friend that I had made in the cadets. Name was May, and he had washed out of pilot training, but had made it in Bombardier School. Saw him and his navigator taken out of the nose of their ship in three blankets. They had taken direct hits of 20-mm shells. My wife asked me in a future letter if I knew a bombardier named May. "Our paper said that he had been wounded."

We also had some excitement that night. A B-17 was up slow-timing an engine. Slow-timing was done with each new engine to break it in. It was done all the time. No one paid any attention, until we heard the prolonged whine of a plane in a dive, then the loud crash and big fire. All three men aboard were killed and we never did find out what caused it. Suicide maybe? They made a vertical dive straight into the ground. Sure made a big hole.

The next day we had a group meeting of our crew and decided to name our B-17. We each put a name in a hat, and we pulled out each one and considered it in turn. The winner was the Sneakin' Deacon. Don't ask why. Guess we thought the name might gain us a favor or two. The name was printed on the plane, and I had Buddy R. painted under my window. Buddy was my father's nickname for our son. Two bombs, for our first two missions, were painted on the fuselage, too, and as we flew more missions, we added more bombs.

Our third mission was to Berlin. At the plane I addressed the bombs "To Hitler—From Doris, Buddy and Hal." There were 660 ships in that raid. Cloud cover at the target was four-tenths, meaning four-tenths of the sky. Of course, at the base we still had the solid overcast.

It was an 800-mile trip each way. There were no incidents until we crossed the enemy coast. Then we started to get flak, light at first, but very accurate. We saw fighters, too, but they didn't get to us because of our fighter support, thank the Lord for them.

We were delivering 5,000 pounds of bombs from 26,000 feet. We dropped chaff, as we always do, to throw off the flak gunners. Chaff comes in bundles, and consists of strips of aluminum that fly all over and are supposed to confuse the flak gunners' radar. It's also called "window" or "carpet." As usual we met the most intense flak on the bomb run. We were flying the number five slot in the lead squadron and taking a lot of hits.

It seemed colder that day for some reason, though the temperature was the usual 40 degrees below zero. There was no heat in those planes. They gave us electric suits to wear, but we didn't, because they could short circuit and then we would really be S.O.L. (no explanation needed). So we were reduced to wearing several layers of clothing. That trip to Berlin wasn't the first. I don't know how many had been made before that but on the first mission there were as many of our airmen killed as there were Germans killed on the ground — 400 each.

We lost two planes on that mission. I didn't know the crews. The trip was ten hours long, with six hours of oxygen (we went on oxygen at 10,000 feet). Back at the base we counted only seven flak holes for all that action. James and I were dead-tired. Ten hours of formation flying is compared to ten hours digging a ditch. But the cold was really the killer, the cold and the oxygen mask.

We were off the next day, so we rested up on the base. I went over to the club and talked to Major "Pop" Dolan. He was the father figure to the group. You could go to him for counseling or advice. Major Dolan had been a World War I pilot and had the wings and ribbons to prove it, but he did no combat flying in this war.

On May 25, we flew to the marshalling yards at Blainsville, France. Again it was overcast in England, but CAVU over France. We flew at 24,000 feet with 5,000 pounds of bombs. It was a six-hour mission. We wore our flak suits and helmet for only about half an hour. We carried the flak suit beside our seat. It looked like a baseball catcher's chest protector and had horizontal stripes of lead in it. It was heavy, so we only wore it when needed. Most wore it over the chest but some sat on it. To protect the family jewels, they said.

We saw few fighters, but did encounter heavy flak and a little 20-mm cannon fire. We had flak damage to our number three engine cowling, a gas line broken. Another cowling and an exhaust system were hit. A piece of flak ended up at my feet. That flight took us over London, the White Cliffs of Dover, Dunkirk and Brussels, Belgium.

It was hard to keep track of crews that got shot down. We didn't go out of our way to find out, mostly because we didn't want to know. But we heard the numbers. We had only completed four missions, but of the last 14 crews shot down, nine were from our squadron. There were only five crews left of the 544ᵗʰ, including us.

Lieutenant James had a sort of telegraph system that his classmates had set up to get information on other crews that left Dyersburg with us. We got word through that system when Seaman's crew went down.

We were then in what was designated the Fourth Phase of the air war. In it, and in Phase Five, we concentrated more of our effort on targets that would benefit our ground troops when the invasion came. We could see ahead to D-Day. It is our time now, but on and after D-Day it would be their time. Everything we had done, all the lives and planes lost, had been with one aim in mind, to make a safer, more successful landing for those men.

With a name like "Sneakin' Deacon," how could we lose? At least that's what the crew thought when the name was suggested.

Harold Rochette's co-pilot seat was named for his son, who was nicknamed Buddy by his grandfather.

Chapter Nine

Mission Five
Is a Rough One

On May 27, we were called for our fifth mission. We had the day before off, so we were quite rested. We were rested, but when I looked at Doc Watson, Bronstein and James, I saw in their faces that the grind was beginning to tell. They looked even worse after this mission.

We went to Mannheim, a railroad center, and dropped 5,000 pounds of bombs. The weather was CAVU with haze. The trip was "only" a six-hour affair, but like most of those affairs it was frought with danger and death. We encountered heavy flak on the way to the initial point where we would turn onto our bomb run.

The flak increased to extra heavy and filled the whole sky. We flew violent evasive action. Two of the planes in the group in front of us went down, one in that familiar corkscrew spiral. I saw the chutes of the tail gunner and a waist gunner bloom from the B-17 nearest to us. We received considerable bouncing around and a

Planes don't fly far after a hit like this.

lot of hits. A survey of the crew produced reports that were all good, just a bunch of holes. The real trouble was yet to come. Fighters, Me-109s, and FW-190s.

First they stood off and peppered us with 20-mm cannon fire, then some came in from about six o'clock high in single file. They held their fire until they were only a few yards away and couldn't miss. They only had enough cannon shells for a few seconds of firing. The ones not firing cannons were using their machine guns. Seemed like hundreds of them. I could see only what was happening in front of me and to the sides. It was rough. We were being pushed all over the sky. Ships were dangerously close to each other at times.

On the intercom all I could hear was hollering, "Bogie at three o'clock high, enemy at ten, level." James was flying the plane. I switched the radio to hear what was going on out there. As if I couldn't see.

I heard the commander in the lead plane scolding the pilots of planes in the group. "Tighten it up number three in the low squadron, you too, number two. Number four in high squadron pull it up, you're lagging." The lead plane had a general riding in the copilot's seat directing operations. The copilot rode in the tail gunner's position and kept the general informed as to the status of his formation.

Our P-47s and P-51s came in to get the enemy off of our backs, but there were too many. While they were engaging one in a dogfight, ten others would jump on the bombers. Back on interphone, I could hear our crew calling out the positions of enemy planes. By now the floor at their positions was littered with 50-caliber shell casings. Cabin air was a blue-gray with gun smoke and I could smell the smoke in my mask. It was being taken in by the automatic intake that mixes cockpit air with the oxygen.

Planes were going down all over the sky. Most of them were out of control, some on fire, some in the familiar spiral, some in a slow roll, until they were upside down and went into a sickening dive, fighters and bombers alike. There were 15 chutes, by my own count, in the air at one time. Brown chutes of the Germans being far out-numbered by the white chutes of the Americans. But those were the chutes of survivors. There were many more that would not be used by others on those lost planes. There was one advantage of flying a fighter, if you were alive you could get out, most every time.

Planes were spinning or diving in, a half dozen at a time, fighters and bombers alike. It was something to see. I wondered how I'd be able to get it all down right in my diary when, and if, I got back to the base.

One B-17, badly shot up and a propeller wind-milling, fell behind. The fighters jumped on him and mauled him badly. His wingman started to drop back, to help protect him, but the lead plane ordered him back in formation. You couldn't jeopardize the safety of the formation even for a buddy. That bomber was lost.

The fighters would come in, shoot us up, roll over and peel off. They killed and wounded a lot of men in planes that were not shot down. But in planes that did get shot down, not all fliers died. Some were badly wounded, some were unhurt, but most were taken prisoner. Some escaped and got back to England, some got messages back, even though they were captured. One such formed the slogan for our group with his message,

"Keep the Show on the Road."

When we got back to the base we left the plane quietly, didn't speak, and didn't check for damage. As we entered for de-briefing I felt weak in the knees and jittery, like I used to feel before a football game when I played. But this was after, not before. This time I needed those two shots of scotch more than anything in the world. They told us 93 German fighters had been shot down.

It was at this de-briefing table that Doc turned to me and said, "If I get through this thing alive I will never leave my hometown again." I'm sure he stuck to it because 40 years later, we tried, Bronstein and I, to get him to come to group reunions. He refused, every time, even though we offered to pay all of his expenses. Later in life, Doc became sheriff of his town, and then mayor. He married, and both he and his wife died before 1997.

After that mission, after we regained our composure, we were told that if we finished our missions and signed up for another tour, we'd make captain. No thanks, we were ready for the flak house now.

Chapter Ten

The Glide Bomb
and Germany's Praise

Each B-17 had its own ground crew consisting of a chief and two or three mechanics. There were also other men who serviced planes as needed, for gas, bombs, patching holes, and so on. The whole base was serviced by 100 mechanics and two officers. It was hard on crew chiefs that had their planes shot down. Some had lost several planes in a short period of time. My guess is that they always had this question on their minds: Was my plane as good as I could make it?

Crew chiefs, and their crews, worked long hours and odd hours. No unions or overtime pay here. Some wouldn't even take leave because they wouldn't leave their planes in another's hands, even for a short time.

It took many people to operate a bomb group and keep the planes in the air. Each base was a small town, with just about everything that a town has, including police and fire departments, a hospital, bakery, restaurants, laundry and social clubs.

We got to know the police department. James had a call from a sergeant at the MP office. Our right-waist gunner had been picked up for brawling and they had him locked up. We were told, "If he has to fly, let us know and we'll bring him up." That happened several times. They picked him up after each mission and locked him up again. The gunner was from the Bronx, in New York City. A burley Irishman with a sense of humor, when sober. He told us that the flak was getting to him and he thought that he should go to the "flak house" for a rest period. He didn't go. None of us ever did.

Sergeant Brown, our radioman, was probably our best candidate for a stay in the flak house. Our crew, his roommates, told us that he'd stay up nights holding his 45-caliber Colt and looking out the window, even after a long, tiring mission. We reported it but that was the end of it. He was very quiet and acted strangely for the rest of our tour. Next August, back in the States, he couldn't recognize me face-to-face.

By that time we were seeing signs of the coming invasion. More servicemen were around, and more traffic. The Allies tried to convince the Germans that the invasion would take place somewhere other than the intended spot. Rubber decoys were in abundance. Rubber balloon tanks and trucks of full size were put in places where German observers would report them, hundreds of them. General Patton was seen with them, lending credence to the illusion.

Deception had been used many times before in the war. The British built a dummy airfield to decoy the Germans away from their real fields. It had hooded runway lights that were lit at night. The Germans bombed it with dummy bombs. A playful sense of humor, even in war.

Our sixth mission was to Cologne, Germany. It was CAVU over the continent, but again overcast at the base. The clouds made us climb to 15,000 feet before we could assemble. After briefing, we were told that we were making history. We, as a group, had been selected to try a new method of bombing. We would each carry one bomb, outside under the wings. It was a 2,000-pounder and it had a wing. It also had twin vertical stabilizers at the tail. It looked like a small B-25. On top, and in the middle of the wing, was a gyrocompass.

We put our formation into a steep glide to get our speed up to about 220 mph. Aiming at the city of Cologne, we released our bombs about 14 miles or more from the target. It was supposed to get us out of the heaviest flak. Maybe it did, because flak was light and not too accurate. We met no fighters, almost like a milk run. After the previous day, any mission would be a milk run.

A general was leading us and commended us for a job well done. We left the city burning in about 20 different places. As we turned off from the bomb run, for the first time I was able to see our bombs explode. But, unlike it sounds, the mission was not a success. The bombs, at 220 mph, were supposed to glide into the target. Some of them did. But others couldn't maintain the glide at that speed. They dropped straight down until they picked up enough speed, then took off in whatever direction they were headed. The gyro held them on that course until they hit the ground. We must have bombed everything within a 100-mile radius.

It was also a costly mission. Many engines on the B-17s were pushed beyond their limit. So many had to be changed that they never tried it again. The extra drag, created by the airfoil of the external bomb, was just too much on so long a haul.

We were scheduled to fly again the next day. The mechanics worked all night repairing and changing engines. There was much talk about the cost, in dollars, of yesterday's mission. It is stated that in war, in the days of the Romans, the average cost to kill a soldier was 25 cents. In World War II, it rose to $25,000 for each soldier.

When they uncovered the map at the front of the room a real deep groan went up. The target was to be Pozen, Poland, a Focke-Wulf plant. The groan was for the time and distance to be flown, 2,000 miles and about 12 hours. It was a torturous journey, on oxygen for so long, at 40 degrees below zero, and flying formation. This was our seventh mission. We were almost a quarter of the way through our tour of 31 missions.

Back when the number of missions a crew was to fly had been decided, the losses in planes per mission averaged out to 4 percent. Some Einstein figured out that at that rate any crew should be shot down in 25 missions, when the 4 percent would grow to 100 percent. In our case, the average loss had dropped a little, so they added on six missions to bring the kill rate back to 100 percent.

For once there were no clouds over the base. It was also CAVU to the target, with haze. We were carrying 2,780 gallons of gas (6 pounds per gallon) and 5,000 pounds of incendiary oil and rubber bombs. The B-17 was designed to fly at a gross weight of 33 tons. We were flying them at 36 tons.

Flak was meager on the way in but we did encounter fighters. Sergeant Sarver, our left waist gunner, swung his gun around too far while tracking an Me-109. He shot off half our horizontal tail surface. I told him on intercom that he should have stayed back in Montana herding sheep. We were flying number two in the lead squadron. The number three plane, to our right, pulled out of formation for no apparent reason. The pilot was looking at me and sort of saluted as he pulled away. He got out about 100 yards and flew parallel with the group. He did so for a few minutes and then just blew up in a red ball of flame. There were no chutes.

We hit our IP and started the bomb run. Flak got a little heavier, but not much. We completed the run, dropping the bombs on the signal of the smoke bomb from the lead plane. When we left the target we saw smoke rising to 20,000 feet from 115 miles away. Fighters hit us again on the way out.

That day the Germans lost 100 fighters, 62 to our bomber gunners. We lost 35 bombers and 11 fighters. It was a long trip. It was cold and our oxygen masks froze up from the condensation of our breath. Our faces and eyes burned from the gun powder smoke.

When we got down to 10,000 feet we took off the masks. Those of us who smoked lit up. We couldn't smoke above that altitude because there wasn't enough oxygen for a cigarette to burn or a match to light. Bob James didn't smoke so he had to suffer through the haze and smell. He never complained though. That's probably why he's still alive today. Not because he didn't complain but because he didn't smoke.

We were very low on gas. We were approaching

"Bombs Away!" Doc Watson yelled that phrase on every one of the
Sneakin' Deacon's 31 bombing missions. In the photo, bombs are
dropping from the lead plane. Note the smoke bomb on the far right.

the channel and letting down. Three planes in our group were letting down faster than the rest of us. They were out of gas and had to ditch. We never heard how they made out. When you ditch in the channel, and survive, it's a race between the British and the Germans to see who gets to you first. About 35 percent of the crews that ditched were saved.

We put over 1,000 planes in the air that day. We flew four missions in five days and had over 40 combat hours on those missions. We were completely exhausted. Colonel Smith spoke on the radio "to let the world know what the 384th was going through. The impossible display of stamina and courage being shown." He further stated that "the 384th was now among the most heavily decorated units in history."

It didn't take a college professor to figure out that it took as much luck as it did skill to stay alive. When we first arrived and talked to the two pilots who lived in our barracks, one of them put it right. "You take your chances," he said, "it's like a lottery. If your number is picked you go down. Sort of a reverse lottery, I guess, an 8th Air Force lottery."

There were figures to back him up. Over 4,500 B-17s were shot down in Europe and another 2,000 written off due to damage and accidents. And those were just the B-17s. A lot of planes were lost due to freak accidents. In one case, a bomb group dropped the bombs on a group below them, causing losses. In another, a B-17 chewed the tail off a sister ship; the plane dove in, and all were killed. There were many mid-air collisions.

There were also a lot of B-24s lost in the 8th Air Force. The B-24 could fly farther than the B-17, but its ceiling was 5,000 feet less. It was bad in propwash, and because of its narrow Davis wing didn't have the staying power of the 17. B-24 crews flying out of Italy got credit for two missions if they crossed over a certain line. In many cases they got credit for two, even when their flight was shorter than some of our longer ones.

In spite of the losses we got the job done. After the war, Germany's Minister of Arms, Albert Speer, said, "The B-17 won the war for the Allies." His statement, in 1945, was supported by Hermann Goering, head of the *Luftwaffe*, who said, "Without the USAF, the war would still be going on, but not on German soil." German Field Marshall Albert Kesselring stated, "Allied Air Power was the greatest single reason for Germany's defeat." All that praise for aircrews who were being piloted by men (and boys), most of whom were civilians just a year before, and at least one who was not old enough to have a drivers license in his home state.

Crews must have sweated out every move of their pilots who only a few months back had never seen the inside of an airplane. Pilots like James and me.

Chapter Eleven

Marathon Flying and Benzedrine Tablets

We were so busy flying we didn't even have time to learn about the other crews with whom we were flying. How were we to know that we were in the distant company of future Senator Barry Goldwater, Jimmy Stewart and Tom Landry (Dallas Coach), all pilots or co-pilots. Never did meet any of them. Never met Clark Gable, a gunner, either.

May 30 turned out to be another clear day, CAVU. The target this time is an airfield and an assembly plant at Halberstadte, Germany. I'm not at all sure of the spelling of some of those names. If I knew the spelling at the time I'm not sure how I put it down in my diary because we were dopey from taking Benzedrine tablets to keep us awake. At first, the tablets were issued to us individually. A gunner on one of the crews took one to stay awake for a scheduled mission. Then the mission was scrubbed and he took a sleeping pill and went to bed, only to be called back because it was on again. He took another Benzedrine and ended up in the hospital. After that, the squadron commanders gave the tablets to pilots only, to be issued to the crew.

We flew our fifth mission in six days, something unheard of. Three months prior, that would have qualified us for a week's rest in a flak house. That was then, this is now.

We were dead tired. The most rest that we had had between any missions was four hours. The tablets kept us awake, but we were logy and slow to react. It seemed as if our minds told our hands what to do and they did it a few seconds later.

We met average flak on the way in and were attacked by Me-109s. They shot down a ship to our left. I saw four chutes in the air. A ground rocket also hit our group. We discharged chaff from the IP to the target as always. The target was destroyed, according to later reports, by direct hits with general-purpose (GP) bombs.

We were falling asleep at the de-briefing. The doctor ordered, "No more flying till you get some rest." So we had our first full night's sleep in four days, and the next two days off.

In the morning I rode to the flight line and talked to some of the ground crews who were waiting for their ships to return. One chief told me about a ball turret gunner who had a 20-mm shell rip through the heels of both his boots. One boot was almost completely torn off. Sometimes those shells exploded on impact and at other times they came right into the plane intact. The gunner escaped unscathed.

That crew chief also told me that Colonel Smith

had started a ground men's orientation program. Ground officers would fly on a mission to get a better understanding of what the flyers were going through. There were some of those observers on the trip that Bob Johnson was on, and one went down with Johnson's ship when all were killed. That ended Colonel Smith's orientation program.

I left the flight line and rode my bike up to the officer's club. A poker game was in progress and I watched it for awhile. There were about three kinds of money in the game besides traveler checks and personal checks. I was invited in but declined, didn't know enough about the values of the monies to make change. I was also mulling over another thing the chief had told me.

He said that some of the crew that Johnson was breaking in with, as its copilot, were on their last mission when they were shot down. All died, including the observer. In addition to the observer, a sergeant had been aboard, flying an extra mission. Before takeoff, headquarters sent word that he'd been given credit for an earlier mission that was questionable. He didn't have to be there; he was through with his tour. He flew anyway.

The next day James and I took a ride to the flight line to watch the planes return from a mission. They had met stiff resistance and had lost three of 18 ships. Several were shooting red flares, indicating wounded aboard, "have ambulance meet us." Red flares meant that Uncle Sam would probably have to pay for some more haystacks. The U. S. had an agreement with England that required payment for damage done to property. I think the local farmers sat by their haystacks with a box of matches, and when a flare was shot off they'd light the haystack and put in a claim. They probably collected a number of times for the same haystack.

Uncle Sam was also charged a fee for each plane that landed or took off, and he paid a tariff for each gallon of gas that came into the country. Those things all came out in the scuttlebutt. After the war, I learned from some combat infantrymen that the same rules applied in France for trees, bushes, and other things.

Lieutenant James went back to the mess hall for dinner. I took a ride into Geddington and had some poached eggs on toast at that one-room restaurant in a house. The menu at the base didn't appeal to me. Every other day it was pork chops and Brussels sprouts, and this was one of those days. A month later, tell that to the infantrymen in France, and they'd say I was crazy. Believe it or not my favorite dish at the mess hall was pea soup with croutons. The croutons were cut from bread that was baked in the base bakery, and the bread was made from the whole kernel of wheat. Nothing was wasted. Have to be careful when you have pea soup, though. If your stomach isn't right, and you have to go on a mission, stay away from anything that produces gas. I'll explain more a little later.

The lady in the restaurant recognized me from a previous visit. The English started liking Americans more than they did at first. Their opinion six months back was "overpaid, oversexed, and over here."

On June 2, 1944, we flew our ninth mission to Neufchatel, France. For a change it was a milk run. Where we expected intense flak and some fighter attacks, we met neither. Again, the weather was CAVU, but undercast at the target. The target was howitzer emplacements and shelters in back of the West Wall. We were carrying 6,000 pounds of GP bombs. A ground rocket missed us by a matter of a few feet. If a ground rocket hits, it'll blow your plane to pieces. That could have been what brought down Bob Johnson's plane about three weeks back.

Because of the undercast, the lead plane, on whose signal we dropped our bombs, was sighting the target with Gee equipment. I don't know how it works, but it's said to be able to put the bombs in a pickle barrel, even through the clouds. There were so many Forts and Lib's here that we had to wait for an opening to the corridor to get out. The corridor is like a channel through known flak gun positions. On the return trip we had a good look at the White Cliffs of Dover again.

We stood down the next day, the third of June. They weren't being kind to us, just resting us up for the big push. They now had us carrying gas masks and wearing our 45s while on the base. There was a possibility of enemy paratroopers dropping in, and they wanted us prepared. The vacation was over! In the next ten days we flew nine missions. We didn't know it at the time, but the run was to start two days before D-Day and carry on from there. We felt better now than we were going to feel for a long time.

On D-Day, minus two, we went after gun emplacements in back of the West Wall. It was overcast with fog at the base, and there was two-tenths cover over the target. We knew D-Day was getting close. It was reflected in the choice of our targets. Missions were designed to help our invading soldiers. All missions had been for that purpose, of course, but these targets were close in. Targets that could hold up the invasion.

We taxied out to the runway carrying 12 500-pound armor-piercing bombs. We were first to take off, so the tower asked if we could see the end of the runway. The fog didn't allow us to see the far end of the runway in front of us, so James looked back over his left shoulder and said, "Yeah, I can see the end of the runway."

We didn't want the mission scrubbed, not after we had come this far. We were supposed to be able to see the far end of the runway before taking off. The normal 30-second interval between planes would be stretched to 60 seconds because of the fog. The takeoff would be more on instruments than visual. After I locked the tailwheel, James pushed the throttles forward. He controlled them all in one grip of his right hand. The props were set at 2,500 rpms and we lifted off at 115 mph. At liftoff I gently hit the brakes, to stop the wheels from spinning before I put them away, and we climbed at 140 mph to the buncher beacon for assembly.

It was a six-hour mission and we bombed from 25,000 feet. We knew it would be a short mission when we saw the gas load, 1,700 gallons. When we got over the channel the gunners test-fired their guns. With all those bombers, we used several tons of lead for that purpose.

On the intercom I called Brown, our radio operator. We wanted to keep a finger on him because of his unusual behavior. We needed him to be alert and perform his duties as required.

At one time there was a gun in the radio-room skylight, which was open, and the radioman manned the gun. But, because of the wind and the limited visibility from that position, the gun had been taken out. The radioman's skills as a radioman were now needed only in the lead plane. Other radiomen acted as spare gunners, if needed, and as first-aid men when required. They also carried spare oxygen masks and toolboxes. Their only other duty was to check the bomb bay after the release. That day we bombed with the Norden bombsight with undercast at only two-tenths.

Flak was moderate but accurate. We saw no fighters but had to put up with a few ground rockets. They must have been saving the fighters for D-Day. They were expecting D-Day, too. Our main concern today was contrails. They are pretty to see but dangerous to fly in. We not only had the contrails from our own group to contend with but also the ones from the groups ahead of us.

If we had to have contrails, this day was a good day to have them. Contrails are like clouds. They're caused by the propellers of the bombers churning up the moist air. Moisture from the engines also helps. There was danger of the bombers running into each other in the soup. There was even more danger if enemy fighters were around because we had to disperse and in doing so would lose some of our protective firepower. No problem that day, though. No fighters. The temperature was relatively mild, only 27 degrees below zero.

Temperatures were always given in Celsius, but when the temperature got down to minus 40 degrees, both Celsius and Fahrenheit are equal on a thermometer and read the same. Below that point Celsius will drop faster. Don't ask me why we needed both readings.

We dropped our 12 500-pound armor-piercing bombs and headed back. We were carrying some ice that we'd picked up when flying through the clouds and contrails, so we got down to a warmer altitude a little faster than usual. Since it was a shorter mission than usual, we got back to Grafton-Underwood early in the afternoon. Because of the short mission and the daylight that was left, our squadron commander, Colonel Nuttall, had me checked out as first pilot. It was a simple procedure, a matter of shooting a few landing and takeoffs with a check pilot, Bob James in this case.

A short time later I was offered my own plane and crew, as a first pilot. I could see no advantage to that. It meant taking on a whole new crew and an untested, inexperienced copilot. I thanked them, but declined. James and I had worked very well together. That had already been proven a number of times and would be proven again in the future. Lieutenant James didn't ask me to turn it down, but I could see that he was pleased when I did. It was a matter of survival.

We didn't know what kind of losses we were taking in either aircraft or personnel. It was a good thing to keep quiet. It wasn't until well after the war that we learned that the 8th Air Force had suffered over 50,000 casualties, with 43,742 killed or missing. That was more than our other eleven overseas air forces combined. It was almost as many as the whole United States Navy lost in the war (46,469). It was also more than all of the marines that were killed in the war (25,386). All U.S. forces combined lost 293,986. The 8th lost over 15 percent of the total. It was more than any other single U.S. military unit.

It was June 5, 1944, the day before D-Day. Of course no one knew it, not even Ike, and he was the one to give the signal to go. We were wearing our 45s on the base. We didn't wear them on missions. The only tool that I wore on a mission was a knife I'd purchased back at Dyersburg for $15. It had a 7-inch blade that came to a point and was sharpened on both sides. I was told that it was made from a circular steel ash saw. I considered the knife a tool, not a weapon, because I only intended to use it to cut parachute cords, if I had to bail out and came down in a tree.

We could choose to wear the 45 or leave it in the barracks. It was six of one and a half-dozen of another. If we bailed out wearing the gun, German soldiers could shoot us as soon as they saw that we were armed. On the other hand, as has happened many times, we could be surrounded by German farmers and pitchforked to death. In that case I would prefer to have the gun. Another choice in the 8th Air Force Lottery.

We were up again at 0230 and on our way to Cherbourg, France, for our eleventh mission. Our target was gun emplacements. The clouds were undercast at 1,500 feet with 40 percent cover at the targets. We would bomb from 26,000 feet. The temperature was minus 38.

We were crossing the channel when the cylinder head temperature on number two engine was getting up over 200 degrees. I opened the cowl flaps. It didn't bring it down but it held steady. Ten missions were considered quite a few in this business, so we had worked our way up, and were leading the formation on this one. Again we saw the rockets, and again they were very close misses. The flak gunners were at it again. I don't know where they got all those shells. They seemed to have different methods of bombarding us. One time they'd send a barrage to a predetermined spot, mostly when we were on a bomb run and unable to take evasive action. Another time they'd track us like they were shooting trap or skeet. They were pretty good, considering they got so many hits and they had to shoot about 20 seconds ahead of our formation.

We were on the bomb run when the amplifier on the number two engine went bad again. It had gone bad earlier and we had changed it in flight. This time we were in the heavy flak area. We were able to hold straight and level until we dropped our bombs. We couldn't stay in formation, had to fall out and let number two take over.

Pictures taken by our photo reconnaissance plane showed the target completely destroyed. Our boys on the ground wouldn't have to worry about that gun battery. We trailed the formation home on three engines. We were lucky again, no fighters around. We would have been dead meat.

Lieutenants James and Rochette humorously guard the air base outhouse from German paratroopers, just before D-Day.

Chapter Twelve

D-Day —
the GI's Longest Day

On June 6, 1944, our orderly woke us up with his excited, "Today's D-Day!" It was 0230 again, and we hadn't had enough sleep.

D-Day didn't mean much to us as far as an invasion goes. Every mission we'd flown had been a D-Day. We were glad, however, that the day was finally here. We prayed for the troops on the ground and wished them success. As I told a civic group that I was speaking to 50 years later, "If D-Day had not been a success we could now be halfway through another 100 year war."

Our assignment was to bomb two bridges, 1,300 feet apart, to keep the Jerries from bringing up their troops. The bridges were in Caen, France. One group was briefed before us, and when we filed out after our briefing, another group came in. Their target was enemy communications. We had learned before that leaflets were usually dropped over cities that were to be bombed.

Don't know if it applied that day or not, but before the war was over the 8th would drop 1,444,280,000 leaflets.

The group that was briefed before us bombed rocket installations. They were called no-ball targets and were used to launch V-1 and V-2 rockets. They were always primary targets and always bombed whenever they could be found. In 1944, V-1 and V-2 rockets caused 30,000 casualties in London. About 2,400 V-1 rockets fell on London. V-1 rockets were also launched from German bombers over the North Sea. That was discontinued because the RAF shot down so many of the bombers.

RAF fighter planes played a dangerous game with the German V-1s. They'd fly along beside the rocket, put a wing tip beneath the wing of the rocket and flip it into a dive before it could reach its target. One method that was used to destroy the launching ramps of the V-1 was to load a B-17 with explosives and fly it until another plane would radio control it into the target. The B-17 pilot would bail out as the radio control took over.

Joe Kennedy, President John F. Kennedy's brother, was killed in a premature explosion while piloting one of those B-17s. The V-2 was a much more dangerous weapon because of its vertical entry from the stratosphere to the target. The Germans had plans to launch 52 V-2s every 24 hours from a super launch site under construction. As the Russians overran those test sites any information they obtained on the bomb would not (repeat, would not) be shared with the Allies. It wasn't until the Poles recovered a V-2, intact, and gave it to the Allies that the 8th became informed. Allied bombers then turned those sites into unrecognizable landscape. Allied leaders called it "a loss of German high-technology that could have turned England into a desert."

On that mission we bombed from 16,500 feet, our lowest yet. The cloud cover over the target was ten-tenths. We bombed with PFF and the target was wiped out, clouds or no clouds, in front of our invading troops. General Eisenhower had promised the troops, "If you see any planes in the air today, don't worry, they will be ours." He was right. We saw no fighters, but did encounter moderate flak.

On the way out we dropped down a few thousand feet for a better look at our invasion. Because of the undercast we couldn't see the beaches, but there were some breaks in the clouds over the channel. We saw a lot of boats and invasion barges. They could see and hear us and they took evasive action. We fired flares of the day. You can understand their concern when you realize that the Germans had a number of B-17s that were flyable. They didn't use them that day. At other times they used them to direct fighter attacks. They also used them to drop supplies to beleaguered troops and to ferry, and supply, agents in enemy territory.

We couldn't see what was going on below, but we knew the conditions our troops were facing. The weather was miserable, the waves were high, and the men were as sick as dogs, and had been for quite awhile. Some drowned as they stepped off the landing barges, with packs too heavy, into water too deep. Omaha Beach was the worst. It had the widest beach and the roughest water. It was a big trap with its obstacles, heavy fire, mines, and our men faced the best-trained German soldiers.

Many of the Allies were killed in landing-craft accidents and in bungled plans and bungled operations.

In the first wave, 25,000 troops would storm the beaches. At low tide they were followed by 125,000 more. About 12,000 would be killed or wounded. These men had all been preceded by glider troops and paratroopers, who had themselves been preceded by dummy paratroopers with firecrackers on them that exploded as they descended. This made for a lot of nervous Germans. When the troops got past the beach and its obstacles, they had to face the Atlantic Wall. That meant heavy guns imbedded in cement and General Erwin Rommel, Germany's best, and his wall of steel. As the Allies advanced, they followed the only formula they knew, "Knock it down, capture it and put it back together."

As they started to take prisoners, they put them on the same barges they had landed on and sent them back to England. In two weeks the Allies landed 625,000 men and 200 million tons of supplies. This day they used 5,000 ships and had 11,000 planes overhead. The troops in the initial wave were men that had not participated in any other landing (some will dispute this). It was intentional. Allied leaders thought that inexperienced troops would be less likely to bolt, run or surrender, than men who had been through it before. It made sense in one way. The Germans, in the first two hours, fired 100,000 shells a minute. There were many thousands of Allied targets for those shells. Inexperience was a plus.

Omaha Beach was again the worst. Two thousand American GIs died there. It could have been worse. The German generals wanted Hitler to release the tanks he was holding in reserve. He wouldn't do so until midafternoon. Some called D-Day the biggest blunder in military history. I don't know if they were referring to the

Allies or the Germans, but there are 9,386 Americans buried on a Normandy bluff and 14,000 more that were exhumed and returned to the U.S. Hitler blamed Rommel for the success of the invasion and also for an attempt on Hitler's life. Rommel was given the option of execution or suicide. He was handed a poison and was dead in 15 minutes.

We returned to base without incident and attended de-briefing. After a bite to eat we went to bed. It was still light, England had only a few hours or darkness at that time of year. After three hours of sleep, we were up and on our way again, for our thirteenth mission.

We bombed a crossroad that the Germans were using to bring up troops. We bombed through eight-tenths of cover from 20,000 feet. The crossroad was in the town of Cande, France. It was a little ticklish bombing in front of our troops, but we were using Gee equipment and our people had a lot of faith in it.

The German Air Force hadn't shown up again, but we expected them at any time. We knew they had over 2,000 fighters in the area. Fewer clouds were over the beaches and channel and we had a front-row seat to the biggest event in the history of the world. The water was full of all kinds of ships and boats, some headed to the beach, and others headed out. The beach, and the land in back of it, was full of shell holes. There was a lot of mechanized equipment on the beach and inland, some moving, others that looked wrecked, some lying on their sides. We could also see what looked like docks that had been moved in. We shot flares, color of the day, to let the ships know that we were friendly.

Back at the base we had to let down through 6,000

feet of clouds, on instruments. We practically held our breath going up or coming down through the soup. So many planes, in so little space, and zero visibility.

We hit the jackpot. We came out right on our base leg and made our approach. We were on the ground two minutes after breaking through the clouds at 2,500 feet. A few hours later we again followed the usual procedure— three hours sleep, then up, shave, Benzedrine tablet and on to breakfast and briefing.

At briefing the faces of the assembled pilots looked haggard. Navigators and bombardiers had their own briefing. Most of them were boys only a few months ago, now they were tired men. The nervous cheerfulness that used to be present at briefing is gone, replaced by quiet. The kid that entered pilot training, too young to have a driver's license in his home state, now looks like a 40-year-old truck driver that's been on the road too long.

All of us walked on our heels, in a leaden gait. We called it the Benzedrine shuffle. After we were back in the States I tried to find Benzedrine in the dictionary. It wasn't there. Maybe I spelled it wrong.

One of our crewmen asked Bob James about non-combat status. He had been told that a transfer to non-combat status could be made, with no stigma attached. He asked, but he never pursued it.

Our fourteenth mission was to the middle of France to knock out a highway and a railroad bridge. The cover would be 50 percent. It was our fifth mission in five days, our sixth in seven days, our tenth in 12. We had flown in 12 days the number of missions that normally would have taken over a month. We met heavy flak and rockets, but our biggest danger was contrails. They were more dense than any that I had ever seen. Real pretty but also real dangerous. We dropped 6,000 pounds of GP bombs. Don't know the results and didn't ask.

On the way out we had our best look at the invasion below. As far as we could see there were boats and barges of all shapes and sizes. There must have been thousands of them. From up in the sky it looked like a person could step from one to another. We were right over the spot of the main invasion. The beach looked so jammed up with tanks, trucks and other equipment that it seemed that the invasion was stalled. I guess the boats below accepted us as friends. They took no evasive action, so we fired no flares.

Back at de-briefing we were again dead tired. I don't know whether we were more dead or more tired. How tired can a person get? I drank the usual shot of scotch but turned down the second one. I didn't know if I could handle it. Our radio operator was about out of his head. James consulted the doctor about getting him into a flak house. He couldn't get him into the flak house, but I think the visit is what got us the next day off.

That night we slept around the clock, and got up still tired. But we weren't the only ones. On a visit to the flight line we found crew chiefs, and their men, in the same condition. Crews were working days on end, catching brief and broken naps on the floors of planes and in makeshift tents. We heard no complaints. They were proud of their work and willing to do what had to be done. They were as proud of their planes as the men who flew them were. One sergeant told me that his ship had returned all shot up, with badly wounded men aboard, and over 100 holes. He said he had already replaced three wing tips and an aileron, two elevators and seven engines. One crew chief bragged of having his plane fly over 50 missions without turning back due to mechanical failure. They were a proud bunch and they let us know it. They'd been there from the start and they told us a lot about the group's history and some interesting stories.

We learned that 20 base personnel were required for every flyer, six of them being line workers. They spoke of an RAF pilot who was still fighting despite the loss of both legs and a German pilot who was shot down twice in the same day. It was from one of them that we learned about The Bloody 100th, a B-17 bomb group that the Germans jumped on every chance they got. It seems that on one of their bombing missions one of their B-17s got shot up pretty badly, fell out of formation and lowered its wheels—a sign of surrender. Two German fighters, one on each side, were escorting him down. After a few minutes the pilot of the bomber corrected whatever problem had caused him to surrender. He ordered the two hapless German planes shot down and returned to his squadron. After that the German fighters exacted revenge at every opportunity.

One mechanic told me about a friend of his who was a tail gunner on a B-17 that flew out of Italy. The man flew on 35 missions and never saw any fighters and never fired his guns. Unbelievable.

We learned that a fully loaded B-17 used 400 gallons of gas an hour while climbing, and 200 an hour cruising. That I could believe, since the average 5,000-plane mission required 200 railroad tank cars of 100-octane gasoline. Before the war was over, the 8th Air

Force would use 1,044,202,050 gallons. Now you know why civilians had to use gas stamps.

Six 384ᵗʰ mechanics, five master sergeants and a T/Sergeant received the Legion of Merit. More flight line info.

As I was riding my bike back to the barracks that night our group was just returning from a mission. It was still light. It didn't get dark until almost 2300 hours. There was a plane on the approach. One engine was on fire and smoke was pouring out of the waist door, which was open. One man bailed out and his chute opened just before he hit the ground. Another followed him, and he landed on a barracks roof and broke it partially through. A third bailed out at too low an altitude. He hit the ground and tumbled along, his chute and its chords trailing. He was about 40 yards in front of me when he bounced up and over a bomb shelter. He rolled another 40 yards and came to rest in a ditch, against a hedgerow, all neatly rolled up in his parachute. He was dead. Had he stayed on the plane he would have lived. The pilot landed it safely.

The "Sneakin' Deacon" crew, minus Sergeant Sarver. Front row: Brown (hand on chest), Smith, Bronstein, Rochette; back row: Kew, Cassidy, Watson, Shay, James.

Chapter Thirteen

New Tactics by Both Sides

The next day we were briefed to bomb an airfield in the center of France. Coverage at the target was 60 percent. Elsewhere it was solid soup from 2,000 to 16,000 feet. We learned that the British had lost 94 planes on their night raid on Nuremberg. Didn't say when it was, didn't matter anyway.

We carried 38 100-pound bombs. Our first task was the hardest; it always was. We had to climb through 16,000 feet of clouds to the assembly point. There we assembled on the spotted cow, a B-17 with purple polka dots on a white background. It was used for assembly purposes only. We headed for the IP while climbing to our bombing altitude, 23,000 feet. About 100 miles in, we got moderate but accurate flak. It bounced us around the sky. We were later told that our bombs hit the field just as the fighters were taking off to come after us. We blew them all over the place. Happy day!

Going home, the ceiling had lowered. We were in the soup down to 300 feet. At that altitude over the channel, we were practically at mast height, in formation, and over navy ships. We all fired flares.

Another plane from our squadron went down this day. We still lost planes regularly, sometimes before we got to meet their crews. The next day, the next mission was a new experience for me. I rode as tail gunner in the lead ship, of the lead squadron, of the lead group of the wing. Lieutenant James wasn't flying. Captain Simon was the pilot and in the copilot's seat was a Bird Colonel. The crew, other than the colonel and me, was Captain Simon's, the 384th's most experienced. My job was to keep track of the 54 planes in back of us and keep the colonel informed. I loved that job. I wasn't expected to fire the machine guns, but I would if I got the chance. I used to be pretty good at trap shooting.

Our target was again an airfield in France. It had a cover of six-tenths, with ten-tenths elsewhere. Five rockets came up and burst nearby. Being in the catbird's seat, I had a much better look at them than I ever had before. Flak could be seen better from the back, too. It was nice being back here, almost like a vacation, no formation flying and the best view in the whole wing. The only movement I really had to make was to put finger pressure on my throat mike. Throat mikes worked on vibration and they worked best if you pressed them tighter. Of course I still had to clear ice from my oxygen mask. One thing I noticed, maybe because I had the time to do so, was how truly uncomfortable the oxygen mask was. It seemed danker and dirtier. Masks required constant monitoring. They could freeze up. They could make you sick, too. I heard of flyers choking on their own vomit.

Before the flight I had taken another tablet. I hadn't had any sleep since the day before yesterday. We saw nothing of the ground on the way back. Only three of the 18 ships from our base were able to get back without getting lost in the soup.

Back on the ground we found out that the grapevine had been active. Five of the crews that left Dyersburg with us, but had gone to other groups, had gone down. Flying so many missions in so few days took its toll on men and machinery, but it paid off. During that period, Germany's oil production was cut back and its transportation system badly damaged.

Our principal opponents in the air war were enemy fighters, flak and bad weather. One of the hazards presented by the weather was frostbite. In the past year it had accounted for more casualties than gunfire, and I am one of them. Even today I have problems with my hands at temperatures below 40 degrees. I like to hunt, and I like go to the Giants' football games in New Jersey. I have season tickets, both Andy Rooney and I. (His seats are probably better than mine.) I have found no gloves that can keep my hands warm enough to dispel that terrible stinging pain when the temperature goes down. But no complaints from me. In the overall picture, where the Air Force dispatched an average of 1,200 aircraft a day, dropped an average of 1 ton of bombs every minute for a year and paid a terrible price, how can one complain about a few sore fingers? Frostbite, however, could be really bad. In some cases hands swelled to the size of boxing gloves and were just as black.

And on we go. D-Day plus six has us on my 17th

mission. The target was a bridge in front of our beach-head. The cover is six-tenths, eight-tenths over England. The load was 8,000 pounds of bombs and 2,100 gallons of gas, total weight of 66,000 pounds. Loaded to the limit. Again we met no fighters, but we did get some heavy flak that tracked us for a long time. We were dead tired, as usual, but the Benzedrine tablets kept us awake. Flak knocked out some engines, not ours, and two bombers dropped out of formation and shot flares asking for fighter escort.

From our recording secretary we found out that ten of the 30 crews that left Dyersburg with us have gone down. That is ten of the 15 that we know about. We don't know where the other 15 are yet. Lieutenant Halbeib, the fellow who gave away the bride at James's wedding, is one of the ten. The way our planes are going down, I'm beginning to see the need for the 160,000 the U.S. produced for the war. Their cost probably accounts for a lot of the $36 billion worth of E bonds that were sold.

The next day we flew our ninth mission in ten days. Still on Benzedrine, of course. Again it would be an airfield, at Dreux, France. The weather at the target is CAVU. Over England, it's zero zero. We bombed from 20,000 feet in the most accurate flak that we have seen to date. All ships were throwing out chaff, but it didn't seem to help. None of the bursts seemed to be farther away than 50 feet. A lot of it was right in front of our ship, and we were flying right into it. How could they be so accurate from 4 miles below?

We picked up over 100 holes. Some pieces of flak probably went right through the ship and made two holes. Back home, we had to go down as low as 100 feet to find the field, in visibility of less than half a mile. I'd rather face the flak than that kind of flying.

We, and other ships, had wounded aboard. There were a lot of flares in the air as we landed, and on the ground they were calling for blood donors. We had flown the lead, in the low squadron of the lead group. We were working our way up.

The following day they stood us down, so Dave Bronstein and I took a ride around the neighborhood, first to Brigstock and then to Geddington. Geddington's claim to fame is the Eleanor Cross. It's about 50 feet tall and looks like a church steeple with indentations in it. It didn't look like much, but it must be famous because about 40 years later my wife and I were part of a tour group that made a special trip to see it. It's directly in front of the Star Pub, which we deemed more interesting.

In the Star, Bronstein and I met an MP named Lee that I had talked with on a previous visit. He was a tall, gangling young fellow from Arkansas. Looked like the typical country bumpkin, acted like one, too. Also looked a little high. He asked if we had seen the flyer bail out over the base yesterday. We said, "No," so he told us. "He was wearing a parachute, which was good, but it didn't open, which was bad, but he was headed for a haystack, which was good, but there was a pitchfork in the haystack, that was bad. He missed the pitchfork, that was good, but he also missed the haystack." At that point Bronstein broke in, "Yeah we know. That was bad." We walked over to the bar and ordered a beer. We didn't buy him one.

While in the Star we listened to a German radio broadcast, Lord Haw-Haw, I think it was. He was telling us where the best spots to visit in England were. He was directing his remarks to the new replacement crews that were arriving. He called them by name and told what groups they were reporting to. Just showing us how good their spy network was.

Lee, the bumpkin, joined us at the bar. He was pretty much under the weather. I told him that he had better cut loose before his buddies had to escort him home. His response was, "I don't shive-a-get, that's pigeon English." That did it. That was the straw. Bronstein and I left the pub, left some change on the bar. Some of the coins were English pennies, big as a U.S. half-dollar. When I left the 384th to come home, I left a drawer half full of those pennies. Too heavy to carry.

The next day we were on call again, this time to hit a viaduct in France ahead of our troops. The hit would stem some of the German reserves coming up to the invasion front. We met flak, as usual, and Lieutenant Summerville and his crew went down, along with another crew I didn't know. In addition two tail-gunners were killed and another wounded. Seems as if those German gunners were improving with all that practice. Wished we could get, as a target, the factories that made their shells.

Some of our other groups must have dropped incendiary bombs in front of us. The weather was CAVU, and we could see French towns burning. Must have been a dozen of them. From 15,000 feet on that clear day, we could even pick out details.

That day we led the high squadron in the lead group. Leading required more work, and it was harder to maintain position. Flying off of a plane that's right next to you is much easier. You can make small corrections early. It was our tenth mission in 12 days and it was a maximum-effort (ME) mission, meaning that everything the 8th Air Force had was up. We lost a 48-hour pass because of it.

The incendiaries we dropped that day were part of the 4,377,984 that the 8th dropped during the war. A group of B-24 Liberators were in the air about a mile to our right. They were silhouetted against some white cumulus clouds. They didn't present near as pretty a picture as a B-17. A B-17 pilot once said that "the B-24 used to be a banana boat, but it leaked so bad, they put wheels on it and flew it." Their crews, however, swore by them and were as attached to their planes as we were to ours. We learned later that they missed their target on that mission.

The 8th was always looking for new ways to combat the enemy and on that mission they tried another experiment. To our Bendix chin turret, which is right under the nose of the plane, they added four more 50-caliber machine guns, in addition to the two already there. They only installed them on one ship, and since we were a lead plane, we got the nod. The purpose was to protect the group in attacks from 12 o'clock. The pilot would fire the guns, all six at the same time, with a button installed on his wheel. He could make small corrections, to line up according to the angle of the attack.

James had his opportunity to be a fighter pilot but he never got to be an ace. It fizzled. When he fired the six 50-calibers there was so much recoil that the plane slowed down considerably, so much so that the rest of our formation shot by us. That experiment, like the one with the "grapefruit" bombs under the wings, was a one-shot deal.

Another experiment involved loading a B-17 with 20,000 pounds of explosives. Another plane radio-controlled it and flew it directly into the target. Much like the Kennedy mission. We weren't involved in that one. so I don't know the results. It couldn't have been very good because it was another one-shot deal.

The 8th Air Force was not the only one looking for ways to improve their attack. The Germans had a few things up their sleeves, too. They were working not only on new planes, and modifications to existing ones, but also on new tactics to exploit them. Two of the new planes that they were producing were the Me-262 fighter and the Arado 234 bomber. Both of those new planes were jets. Both used engines that were good for only ten hours. The manufacturers couldn't get the proper metal for the job and had to use steel. In spite of the handicap they built 1,200 Me-262s, and during their limited use they made over 700 kills.

German airfields were being pounded pretty heavily. That forced the Me-262 fighters to use highways for landing strips and bridges for hangers. The tactic came to mind many years later when the U.S. was building its interstate highway system. Plans specified that at least one mile in every five be straight, to allow the highway to be used as a landing strip in an emergency.

It was around that time that the Germans tried to perfect a new type of parachute. It was called a reef parachute. The parachute had a band around it that allowed it to open only part way, but the band could be released for a full opening. It allowed for something between a free fall and a regular parachute fall, and the flyer could control it. The Germans also worked on an ejection seat. Years later the U.S. used the idea on its military planes.

The Germans also built 30 Me-163 rocket planes. They were much faster than anything we could put in the sky. On takeoff, as it was becoming airborne, it would drop its wheels and become a rocket. That was a major problem because many times the wheels would bounce up and hit the plane, causing an explosion. The plane could fly at 630 mph, but it used most of its fuel just to get to altitude. At the end of its flight, the pilot bailed out, so it was a one-shot deal anyway. It was used briefly in 1945. The war ended before the Me-163 and the Arado 234 could be perfected.

Other tactics the Germans worked on at that time could be called desperation tactics. The Focke-Wulf engineers took a standard FW-190, added some armor, much more firepower, and some bulletproof glass, making the plane heavier and less maneuverable. In combat, the planes would be escorted by Me-109s that were modified with more powerful engines and less armament. That formation of planes was called Sturmstaffel One. It was formed for one purpose—to knock down bombers. What else? To pilot the FW-190s, they picked men from different squadrons, men who appeared to be over-aggressive and gung-ho. Pilots with something to prove. Some were in their commander's doghouse.

The commander of that group took a page from the Japanese when he had each pilot sign a statement that he would not return until he had destroyed an American bomber. Even if he had to ram it to do so.

The first time they used that unit to attack American bombers they were pitted against a group of B-24 Liberators. They caught up with the bombers over Leipzig. The Germans split into three groups, and each group attacked from a different direction. They held their fire until they were within 100 yards of the bombers, because they had only five seconds of firepower to work with. In less than one minute from the start of the attack, 18 bombers had been shot down, an entire group. Another ten fell to the fighters. This formation, and its method of attack, was a disaster waiting to happen again and again, unless a defense could be found to defeat it.

The 8th sent up fighters to patrol the rear of the bomber formations, looking for Sturmstaffel formations that were forming for attack on the bombers. Once they dove in and broke up the formations, the Germans could not recover fast enough for a successful attack.

The Sturmgruppe tried these attacks two more times. Neither was as successful as the first one.

Men from the "Sneakin' Deacon" show off their jackets. Each bomb stands for a mission flown by the wearer. Left: Harold Rochette's A-2 jacket. Right: Five members of the crew that flew the "Sneakin' Deacon" when Rochette's crew did not.

Chapter Fourteen

The Lead Banana
and Fighter Pilots

The next day, the 16th of June, we were called up to go to Lyon, France, after another airfield. Cloud cover was eight-tenths over England, six-tenths at the target.

We were leading the low squadron in our group. Flak was moderate and accurate on the bomb run. The lead ship in the high squadron took a near direct hit. Another burst knocked out an engine and the plane did a slow rollover and went into that slow corkscrew spin. I saw three chutes blossom before the ship slid below us and out of sight.

On the return trip I was flying overlap formation with Lieutenant Goddfried, a way of putting the wing tip of our plane in between the horizontal tail surface and the wing of his plane. Foolish but exciting. It had been a long and tiring mission. Ten and a half hours at 20,000 feet, 30 degrees below zero. Flares were being shot over the home base indicating dead and wounded aboard.

Ambulances responded.

Most of what I've written so far has to do with bombers of the 8th Air Force. Not much about fighters.

Let it be said that there was no prettier sight than seeing our "little friends," the fighters, circling out there. Usually they were cautious and didn't point their noses in toward our formations. Smart, too, because over 100 nervous gunners, with itchy trigger fingers, were watching them. Fighter pilots who shot down five enemy planes would earn the title of Ace. Many American pilots qualified, some several times over.

None, however, would come close to amassing the totals that some German and Russian pilots had. Those pilots, especially the Germans, had been flying and fighting for years before America got into the war. German Ace, Major Gerhard Barkhorn, downed 301 enemy planes. Gunther Rall confirmed 275 victories. Otto Kittel accounted for 267 and Anton Hafner for 204. Other notable Aces were: Heinz Baer 220, Anton Hackl 192, Erich Rudorffer 222, and Hauptmann Helmut Lipfert 203. All of those Aces were shot down many times themselves, only to rise and fight again. Only Kittel and Hafner were killed in action. Thirty of Major Baer's kills were B-17s.

The best of the Russian Aces was Major Ivan Nikitich. He shot down 62 German planes, on 520 missions, and was shot down several times himself.

While our little friends didn't square off against the Russians, they no doubt fought against the German Aces. Between them, the fighters and gunners on our bombers accounted for 15,439 kills in the air and thousands more on the ground, all that to protect the bombers while they were dropping 701,300 tons of bombs.

After a day of rest we were off again, this time to Hamburg, Germany, and an oil plant. Coverage at the target would be six-tenths, with the usual ten-tenths over England. It was our twenty-first mission.

After climbing through the overcast, we picked out the correct colored flare and assembled with our group. We carried GP bombs for the refinery. It was a bitter day; the temperature was its usual 40 degrees below zero. As explained before, James and I didn't wear heated suits because they could short out at the elbow. We had no heat of any kind except that which our own bodies generated.

As we crossed the coastline of France, we met rockets and very intense flak, which continued off and on until we got to the IP. My oxygen mask kept freezing up and I had to remove my gloves to unsnap it from my helmet. Then I had to crack the ice loose. My hands had passed the numb stage by the time I had finished. Another contribution to the frostbite that I would suffer.

We used our steel helmets and flak vests more than usual on that trip. We used both when it got intense. From the weight, I assumed that the flak vest had lead strips in it, but I later found out that overlapping plates of titanium steel were sewn into that canvas vest.

On the bomb run, we ran into the worst flak barrage we had seen to date. We learned later that it was the heaviest flak barrage in history. In addition to the flak we were also getting rockets. Between the two, they blew our formation all over the sky. Flak was in bursts of six, and we were in it for over ten minutes.

Engines were smoking and on fire; those that could be were feathered. The lead plane was knocked out and the deputy lead took over. For a short while they had the honor. A direct hit killed the pilot and wounded the copilot. Throttle handles were shot off and instruments smashed. The wounded copilot had to operate the throttles and fly the plane with one hand. He held on and completed the bomb run before he relinquished the lead. Badly wounded, and with only one hand, he was able to stay in formation.

We bombed from 26,000 feet. As we got a good distance away from the target we could see black smoke rising to about 20,000 feet.

For quite awhile I had wanted to write Doris a long letter while on a mission. So while James flew the plane I wrote about what was happening. No way did I expect to see so rough a trip. When I looked at the letter before I mailed it, it looked like the shaky scrawl that I had produced back in the oxygen tank when they had us write our name over and over. I sent it anyway.

We were called out again the next day, the 19th of June, for our twenty-second mission. It had been only 37 days since we flew our first mission. This target was a dual crossroad and rocket installation. We had 38 100-pound GP bombs. The cover was seven-tenths and hazy. The target was in back of Calais and we bombed from 25,000 feet with good results.

Flak made a few holes in our ship. Our wingman and a few others in our group got hit pretty bad. They lost engines and had hydraulic systems shot out. We saw propellers windmilling. That happened when we couldn't feather the props. If the blades were turned into the wind they wouldn't windmill and would cause less drag. That, however, couldn't always be done.

The Sneakin' Deacon, our plane, must have received more flak damage yesterday than we had thought, so we were assigned another ship for this mission, the "Lead Banana." And it flew like it was made of lead. It was the slowest ship in the group and was used only as a spare. We had to pull 2,300 rpm and 42 inches to stay with the group. That was partly due to the extra weight of the camouflage paint. The 8th Air Force quit using the paint in January of 1944 after the Jerries perfected their radar.

The next day we got a four-day pass. We spent those days on what you might call day trips. Using our bikes we traveled to nearby towns and villages. No sense going to London again; we didn't enjoy it much the first time. Anyway, it was more of a rest period than anything else. We visited those standbys, Brigstock, Geddington, and Grafton-Underwood, and took a longer ride into Kettering. Kettering was a city. It had theaters and a railroad station. So instead of planes we watched trains. We were back on the base each day to watch the boys returning from their missions.

It was depressing, but we always seemed to end up down at the flight line. We were getting to know some of the other pilots. Not by sight but by name, names that were on our flight position charts. On one of those days, one of the names that we recognized was coming in with numbers three and four engines out. One was trailing flames and the other smoking. As they were both on the same side of the plane the pilot had to carry that wing high. The good engines on the lower side could provide the lift needed to keep the plane flying. As the plane hit the ground the lower wing dug in and the plane cartwheeled and burst into flames. All on board perished. Accidents like that took place after most missions, but most of them were not nearly that bad.

One thing that bothered us more than anything else was the lack of news concerning the status of our boys on the ground in France. They were having a rough time of it and some of the worst was yet to come.

During the next winter, as the Germans were retreating, they took their Allied airmen prisoners of war with them. In one of the harshest of winters some 6,000 prisoners were force-marched 600 miles in 86 days. Over 1,300 airmen died on the march. In later years, one man told me about life in a POW camp. Little or no food and inhumane treatment from guards who were in almost as bad a condition as the prisoners. His weight dropped from 135 to 80 pounds. Now, 55 years later, tears welled in his eyes as he told me his story.

Bad as that was, it was not as bad as the "death camps." Two GIs who had liberated one of these camps told me of bodies piled almost ceiling high. Bodies that were so thin they could almost see through them. One GI said, "The ones who were still alive were in no better condition. They were all crying. I don't know where they got the liquid for those tears."

His friend added, "We were assigned to clean up the place for some American and German politicians. The stench was terrible. Vomit and body waste was everywhere. We had a week to clean it up and remove the bodies. Too bad the politicians couldn't stand to see, and smell, the raw truth."

Chapter Fifteen

Missions Increased

After four days of standing down we were all well rested and ready to go—to Bremen, Germany, after some oil plants. Coverage was eight-tenths at the target so it would be PFF bombing again. We were carrying 12 500-pound GP bombs and bombing from 27,000 feet. The temperature would be a bit warmer, minus 33 degrees.

We were told at briefing that there would be flak along the way, and at the target there would be 460 flak batteries, each containing four or six guns. You do the math. In addition to all that flak, we met plenty of rockets again. It was rough.

Again we lucked out, and the lottery was working in our favor. Just a bunch of holes. Others got shot up badly. Lieutenant Finch and his crew, our squadron, were lost. No chance to get out. He was the twelfth of the 18 ships in our squadron to go down since we'd been here. Lieutenants Hanson and Filer, from Dyersburg, had also gone down. They made twelve of 17 reported on the grapevine. Most of those crews have only ten to 15 missions, only two-thirds of what we have flown.

There is much discord among the crews at our base. The higher-ups increased the number of missions on us. Instead of flying 25, we now have to fly 31. Only 35 out of 100 crews are making it to the top as it is. With six missions added, that number will decrease.

Somewhere in this time frame the first shuttle mission to Russia was flown. Two bomb wings, the 13th and the 45th flew it. The Bloody 100th was in the 13th wing. The plan was to bomb German targets, land at Pltava, Russia, reload and bomb targets in the Balkans, land in Italy and bomb more targets en route to England. It was not to be. The 73 bombers landed in Russia and the crews were wined and dined by the Russians. That night two German bomber units, Junkers JU-88s, marked the Russian field with flares and bombed for more than two hours, unhindered. The Russians had few antiaircraft guns. Two Americans were killed and six wounded. Of the 73 bombers on the field, 47 were completely destroyed and another 15 damaged. The stranded airmen had to be picked up by Air Transport Command and flown back to England. Only two more shuttles would be flown after that disaster. As our troops on the ground advanced, the German flak guns were being concentrated in a smaller area. We could verify that fact by the amount of flak we were getting.

As many stories as there are in the air, there are just as many or more on the ground. One of the more interesting ones, told to me by a member of the Antique Veterans group, took place in a bombed-out village.

It was well below freezing and the GI and his friends were seeking shelter. They came across a building that had been leveled, only the floor was left. They discovered a trap door, opened it, and descended into the cellar, where they found four dead Germans, frozen stiff. They removed three bodies through the trap door, but the fourth was too big, and frozen in a crouched position. They considered sawing him in half but had no saw. So they did the next best thing. They pushed him up against a wall and used him as a bench.

One unusual story brings another. This one took place in a large bomb crater that some GIs roofed over with planks. They built a roaring fire to keep warm. Every time they added wood to build up the heat, they could smell meat cooking. It wasn't long before the frozen wall in back of the fire crumbled, and a dead German started to show. He was being baked in his own oven.

Strange as these happenings are, the Russians did things just as bizarre. As the troops moved forward they carried their wives, or girlfriends, and their horses with them. They would move into a beautiful marble building with nice oak flooring. The troops, horses and women all in the same area. They would use one corner of a large room as a common toilet for all. Before long all the flies would be in that corner. It was called bunching. It wasn't long before the beautiful floors buckled and the place smelled. When I asked the storyteller what the women looked like, he replied, "Pretty much like the horses."

My friend Dick Egan was one of the very first American soldiers to occupy Berlin. Of course the Russians were there about the same time, and problems arose between the two forces. "The Russians," he said, "were driving their big trucks, three or four of them in train. They'd barrel down the street like a big train and run over every German citizen they could. If they saw Germans on the sidewalk, they'd go up on the sidewalk after them."

To stop the needless killing, the U.S. Army posted an MP, along with a Russian MP, on as many street corners as possible. One Russian MP stopped the practice. According to Egan, the MP pulled over a speeding truck, hauled out its driver, and beat him savagely with a police baton for close to ten minutes. The driver lay there bleeding and the MP hopped back into the jeep and said, "Let's go."

One of our guys asked, "Aren't you going to do anything for him?" and the Russian said, "Don't worry, he won't speed anymore." What was most unforgettable, Egan said, was how the Russians, Germans and Americans left the driver on the road. No one even shut off the truck, so it ran until the gasoline was gone. "They stopped running over people after that," Egan said.

It is now June 25, 1944, and our 24th mission. It is warm up here today, only 22 degrees below zero. I wrote only one word in my journal, "Soup." Our target is a railroad bridge in Sens, France, and we have two 1,000-pound bombs to deposit on it. That ton of bombs represented just one of the 1,940 tons that our group dropped on the area, from the western tip of France to Berlin, in the month of June 1944.

We were meeting light to moderate, but acceptable, flak. We were bombing from 21,500 feet. That probably accounts for the warmer temperature. We were about 5,000 feet lower than on the last few missions. On the bomb run we had a burst of flak at 11 o'clock (when calling positions around the plane we use a clock with the nose of the plane at twelve o'clock). The burst was real close and scared the you-know-what out of Bronstein and Watson.

There were cases where the whole nose was blown off and the bombardier blown out, without his parachute. There was even one time when a gunner was blown out of his own plane and into another. Sounds impossible until you see the damage suffered by some of the Flying Fortresses. Some had holes that a small car would fit through, and the plane would still fly.

When it came time to drop our two bombs, only one would go. We couldn't dislodge the other, so we had to make another trip to the Wash and work it out at a lower altitude. A move that was always tricky.

We arrived back at base at 2300 and watched the fireworks again as the incoming crews called for ambulances for the dead and wounded. Again, we had flown the lead in the high squadron of the high group. We were the real veterans now, with about twice the missions of anyone else in our squadron.

Both James and I began to notice that after each mission it was taking longer and longer to get the buzzing out of our ears. The buzzing was caused by listening to the shrill clamoring on the radio and the roar of the engines. We would both need hearing aids later in life.

When I went to our group reunion I could pick out the pilots by checking their ears for hearing aids. Otherswore them, too, but most of the pilots usually wore two. In later years I wondered if people like Barry Goldwater and George McGovern wore hearing aids. As stated before, both were B-17 pilots, as were the actor Jimmy Stewart and Tom Landry, the Dallas Cowboys' coach. Joe McCarthy was a tail gunner, the same Joe McCarthy that caused all the trouble with his accusations of communism. Three of the men above became senators. In the years after the war, many veterans were elected to Congress. As years go by, however, fewer and fewer veterans are in Washington. They are getting older and dying off. As a result, fewer bills are being brought up, or passed, that favor the military.

The next mission, our twenty-fifth, was a milk run. A short five hours and 15 minutes. The route was only a short distance in to the town of Neufchatel, France. The target was a no-ball, the code name for the ramps that were launching the V-1 and V-2 rockets on London. We were carrying two 5,000-pound GP bombs and dropped them from 27,000 feet. The temperature was 35 below zero. During assembly we had high cumulus clouds over the base. They gave us trouble while we were getting the group together. As this was an afternoon mission, we didn't get back to the base until 2100 (9:00 p.m.).

Other than a few holes in the fuselage, the only other excitement we had was when our tail-gunner passed out from lack of oxygen. His breath had caused the tube on his mask to freeze up. We picked it up on a routine intercom check and rescued him in time.
We had eight-tenths coverage at the base. When we broke through we were over another field and had to sort out our own field. With more than 130 fields in England, it was sometimes hard to find your own, especially in bad weather.

To this point, and through World War II, the Air

Force had been part of the Army and was called the Army Air Force. It didn't become the United States Air Force until July 26, 1947, and then only after President Harry Truman had said, "Air power has developed to the point where its responsibilities are equal to land and sea power."

The Navy's objections were predictable. They were still bristling over General Billy Mitchell's declaration, back in 1921, that its "battleships were obsolete and no longer capable of defending American shores." What made it worse was that he had proven his point by sinking a number of captured German warships and obsolete American ships, by bombing them from the air. For all of his trouble he was court-martialed and broken in rank. He died in 1936, never seeing his dream come true.

We now had flown 25 missions in 45 days. Unheard of until the invasion was in sight. Our group was not the only one going through the grind. Every so often we got a chance to talk to some flyers from another group. Their problems were the same, lack of sleep, Benzedrine tablets, and despondency.

One gunner told me that he feared the flak and rockets more than the fighters. "Against fighters, you can shoot back, but not so against the flak. All you can do is force your way through it. Doing nothing is the problem." He told me he had just passed his eighteenth birthday and had finished his sixth mission. He had always wanted to fly, and took the opportunity when the war came along. I took an interest in him and encouraged him to talk. He was so young to be going through such an obstacle course. He admitted he had considered asking for ground duty, but was too proud to do so.

Overall his opinion seemed to be the same as most other flyers. They all thought that many would be killed, but not themselves. They all figured that the drawing in the 8th Air Force Lottery was in their favor. In spite of everything we knew, we still had our superstitions. Some men carried some sort of keepsake; others had a certain ritual they would follow. Mine was to wear the same clothing on every mission, several shirts, a sleeveless sweater my wife had knitted, long johns, shoes, flying boots, gloves, and heavy jacket. At this point they were so dirty I could stand them in the corner when I took them off. All that, of course, was in addition to our Mae West, parachute harness, flak suit, and helmet.

We had a few days off before our twenty-sixth mission. We figured our ground forces were doing pretty well if our unit could stand us down for that period of time. We spent time at the Officer's Club talking to some British pilots. They told us some things that we probably would not have heard anywhere else. For example, they said the Germans were working on two experiments involving two different planes, the Mistel and the Me-328.

The Mistel was a bomber loaded with explosives, with a manned fighter plane flying piggyback on the bomber. The pilot dove both planes at the target, then released the bomber and flew the fighter plane back home. The pilotless bomber continued on to the target.

That procedure was much like the under-the-wing bombs and the explosive-laden B-17 we had tried. The Me-328 was used in pretty much the same way as the Mistel, except both planes were manned. As they got close to the target the bomb-laden Me-328 would separate from the empty bomber and fly ahead to the target.

The bomber would leave, and the Me-328 pilot would dive his plane toward the target and bail out. He was on his own to find his way back. The bomber had been used as a transport.

The British pilot hadn't seen the experiments in action and didn't know the final outcome. The pilot asked us, "Have you had any children's parties lately?" The Americans would have a party for the kids on any holiday or occasion. I told him we hadn't had any holidays since I'd been here, except for Independence Day, and I added, "I don't think you British would appreciate having your children celebrate that."

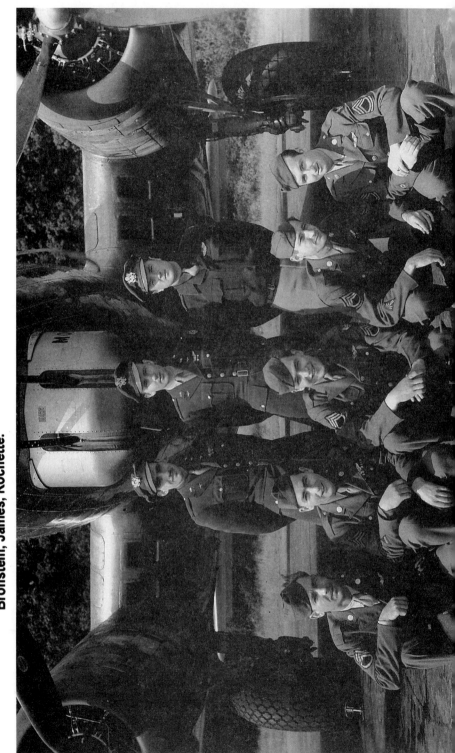

Another photo of the "Sneakin' Deacon" crew, minus Lieutenant Watson and Sergeant Smith. Front row: Kew, Sarver, Cassidy, Brown, Shay; back row: Bronstein, James, Rochette.

Chapter Sixteen

Elwood Slides
for Home

With our "vacation" over we prepared for our next liaison with fate, a buzz-bomb installation in the Pas de Calais area.

At the target, another formation of planes cut in front of our wing. Colonel Nuttal, who was leading our wing, had to dive our whole formation to avoid a mass collision over the target. We circled our formation and returned for a second run, only to find another group making a run on the target. Colonel Nuttal considered things too messed up at that point to make a third run, so he broke our wing into three groups to bomb three secondary targets. Our particular target was an airfield on the French-Belgium border.

We reached the target and, quoting from my journal, "we got the hell shot out of us today by flak." Several ships in our group had their engines shot out. Some were flaming, others smoking, feathered, or their propellers windmilling. Planes were aborting and heading for the coast. There were a lot of dead and wounded. Three on our crew were wounded—Shay our engineer and top turret gunner, Sarver the left waist gunner, and Bronstein, our navigator.

Although our ship took a lot of punishment, and was full of holes, we still had all four engines. One good-sized piece of flak bounced off my flak vest right in the middle of my chest. Good thing I was wearing it instead of sitting on it, "protecting the family jewels." I still have the piece of flak. Didn't know that you could sweat at 35 below. Our three wounded were not serious and could hold on until we returned to base. Good thing, because there are no medics up here. Brown was still flak-happy, but he could handle the smaller wounds. He still had enough of his head left to do that.

Lieutenant Elwood had his number two engine shot out and on fire. A burst of flak exploded in his open bomb bay snapping control cables and smashing radio equipment. He was trying to get back into formation when a third burst knocked out his other inboard engine. He headed for home. But he wasn't out of it yet. As he approached the French Coast he came within range of more guns. A third engine was knocked out. Of the three, he could only feather one, so he had two violently windmilling props threatening to tear his plane apart. He jettisoned his bombs. His crew was throwing everything that was loose overboard to lighten the load on the one good engine.

When Elwood got over the water, his first thought was to ditch. He ordered his crew to assume ditching position, which means everyone but the pilots faces backward, with their backs against a bulkhead. He quickly re-scinded the order, because he decided the risk to ditch was greater than trying to get home. He carried on. His next thought was to land at an emergency field. That thought was abandoned when only one wheel would go down. So he said, "the hell with it. Let's go for broke." He brought the ship back to Grafton-Underwood and belly-landed it with two windmilling propellers, a strong tail wind, and his head out the window, trying to see around the damaged windshield. The plane had over 300 flak holes and several wounded crewmen.

This story got back to his hometown of Chicago and was printed on the front page of the local paper. His wife sent him a clipping. The newspaper had only half the story. The way Elwood told it, it was much more in-teresting. To understand what really happened you must know something about atmospheric pressure and its ef-fect on the body.

If you've ever traveled on a commercial airline, you have probably felt pressure in your eardrums as you ascended. It's caused by the atmospheric pressure de-creasing and the pressure inside your eardrums trying to adjust. You can relieve the pressure by swallowing, yawning or chewing gum. On commercial airlines this correction takes place until you get to a set altitude where the cabin pressure is automatically stabilized at that point for the rest of the ascent. In a B-17 there is no pressurized cabin; you must make corrections all the way up to where the air is rare. If you have a cold and your sinuses are plugged, it's very painful. You might even break an eardrum. The change in atmospheric pressure effects other parts of the body in the same way. The pressure in your stomach tries to equalize by pushing out. The higher you go, the less outside pressure, the more the push.

Now back to Lieutenant Elwood's story, the way he told it. Everything about his heroic effort to bring back that B-17 is true. What he added was this:

He had eaten some gassy food and he had diarrhea. If you have to relieve your kidneys in a plane, you can use a condom or a can, and throw it out the window. Diarrhea is something else. You have to sit in it. Elwood told it like it was, he slid around in it. To make matters worse the oxygen in the plane is not pure oxygen; it's automatically mixed with the cabin air. The intake is right beside the pilot's seat, so the air picked up the smell of the diarrhea. This, added to the sliding around, made his effort all the more heroic. It could have made the newspaper story that much more interesting. Guess there's a bit of humor in almost everything. In baseball terms you could say, "Elwood was sliding for home."

For the next five days the weather kept some of us on the ground. At that time of year, England got about 14 days of rain a month, and when it wasn't raining, clouds were almost down to the ground. The enemy, with all its flak, fighters and rockets, had never turned back any of our formations. Only the weather could do that. Our soldiers and sailors could be slowed down by weather, but not completely nullified.

One of my friends in the Antique Veterans, who served in Italy before going to France, told me that at times they were slowed to a crawl, and it was then that they were the most vulnerable. The Veterans' meetings are teaching me so much about World War II, things that

I would never have known, things that never appeared in the news, some things that were better left unsaid. I would never have known, for instance, that 23 American C-47s full of U.S. paratroopers were shot down over Anzio by befuddled American gunners. It was told by an observer and verified by others.

Private Slovak was the only American soldier who was executed for desertion in World War II, that I knew of. But I didn't know about the soldiers who were executed for rape and murder. Soldiers executed for rape? Compare that to the Japanese Army that forced thousands of conquered women into brothels called Pleasure Palaces.

Of course, our group also tells jokes. In addition to the jokes, there are also humorous stories to be told. Robert Coffey, a Navy veteran, told one of note. His ship had anchored off an island in the South Pacific where the females of the native population wore no clothing from the waist up. When the ship's chaplain saw the half-naked women he thought something should be done about it before the sailors went ashore. He asked the ship's captain to issue white T-shirts for the ladies. The captain did. When the sailors went ashore, each woman was wearing a white shirt—with two grapefruit-sized holes cut in the front to accommodate their breasts. But the funniest part has yet to be told. As the veteran was describing the half-naked women he said, "all the women were bare-ass, from the waist up."

Chapter Seventeen

Bombing My Future Daughter-in-Law

On the morning of July 12, 1944, after our five days of rest, we were awakened for our twenty-seventh mission. After cleaning up, with some of the 20 tons of soap the 8th Air Force used every day, we went to the mess hall and ate some of the 600 tons food that it consumed daily.

The mission was to Munich, Germany, and we had ten-tenths of undercast from base to target. Since we last flew, our group had eight more B-17s go down, and a lot more men killed or wounded. On the ten-hour mission, we would bomb from 26,000 feet. The 8th had 1,200 bombers in the air that day.

Flak was intense, very heavy, and very accurate. Turner's ship in front of us received a direct hit and turned into a ball of orange flame. No one had a chance to get out. Another, to our right, had a hit between the number three and four engines that took out the both of them. It dropped off to the back of us and slid away.

When we returned to base we found out that, in addition to the two planes lost on the mission, we had lost two more on take-off due to a mid-air collision in the clouds. Later in the day we were told that the crews of Pete and Patrick, I never knew their last names, from Dyersburg were down. That made 14 of 22 that we know about and eight that are in limbo.

If it is of any interest, our plane used 2,400 gallons of gas today. All that with no gas stamps. All of this cost in human life, and in dollars, was not for naught. Tens of thousands, probably hundreds of thousands, of Allied Forces and civilian lives were saved due to the bombings of submarine pens, V1 and V2 Launch Pads, oil factories, railroads and many other strategic targets.

The next day we were off again to Munich, our second trip, but the third for the 384th. Coverage was still ten-tenths. That day 1,000 bombers carried incendiary and general-purpose bombs. Flak was extra heavy and accurate, tracking us on both sides. We bombed with PFF from 25,000 feet using the center of the city as the Main Point of Impact (MPI). After the bomb drop, we flew along the Alps and Lake Constance on the way back.

With a ceiling of about 300 feet, we had to drop down on the deck to find the field. It was a bit hairy, with radio towers and so many other aircraft in the vicinity, and visibility only half a mile. It was a ten-hour trip, with seven of them on oxygen. That makes 14 of the last 30 hours on oxygen. Three more Dyersburg crews were down, Bumbartel, Felds and another. The count was 17 of 25 down.

Of course I didn't know it at the time, and would

not find out for another 20-some years, but my future daughter-in-law was down there in Munich. At the time she had yet to be born. Her mother was carrying her in her womb. Rose came to the States with her mother when she was ten years old. While in college, she met my son, who had just finished three years in the Navy.

Many years later Rose told me some of the things that happened to her family during those trying times under Hitler. When she was three months old, they were living in Prussia. Her parents had to pick up coal along the railroad tracks for what little warmth they had. Before that, her family owned a large farm and was considered well-to-do. Her mother had paid the mayor of East Prussia to keep her husband out of the military.

Rose's father was anti-Hitler and had some war-related material that the Gestapo was interested in. When they called, he was not in, so they took his best friend. He was never heard from again. The family was given one hour to move out of their farm. Then times got really hard for them. Rose's mother told her of other mothers leaving their dead babies along the roadside. The Russians took her father, aunt and grandmother. Her father came back four years later when Rose was four years old. He died when she was ten, and Rose and her mother came to America. Her father, of course, was buried in Germany. It is interesting to note that grave sites in Germany are rented for only 30 years. After that period they must be re-rented for another 30 years, if desired.

While Rose (given name Roswitha) was in college at Southern Connecticut State University, our son was in the U.S. Navy. He was honorably discharged in San Diego and hitchhiked home. It took him three days, with no sleep. He was carrying a 30-30 Winchester rifle. That was in 1963. Try that today. His last ride was on a truck loaded with cow manure and it was during the warm summer months.

Our son and Rose now have a daughter who is a senior in high school. She has no knowledge of World War II. History in American schools rarely goes past the Civil War. Her mother, educated here and a teacher with a Master's degree, has little more. She told me that Germany teaches more about World War II than the United States does. She stated, "History in the U.S. starts with the *Mayflower* but runs out of steam many years before World War II."

My cousin, a college professor, told me that American history education ends somewhere about the middle 1800s. Good enough reason to publish this book.

Losses were still piling up, both here and in other groups. Smith, from Dyersburg, had been shot down. Eighteen out of 26. The lottery went on. The 8th Air Force was getting to be the Iwo Jima of the air. Almost 7,000 U.S. Marines were killed there, one-third of all Marines killed in the war. The 8th lost over six times that many.

Losses for the Germans were also piling up. By war's end our gunners shot down 6,001 fighters and our fighter planes got many more. That, in addition to thousands more that were destroyed on the ground. Fighters destroyed by strafing 7,487 freight and oil cars, 4,660 locomotives and 4,882 vehicles. Damaged equipment in those categories totaled another 30,000.

Many decorations would be presented to Air Force flyers in the 8th for conspicuous gallantry and risk of life. Andy Rooney, a journalist who flew a mission on a B-17, said that, "the Air Force liked to hand out medals." He then added, "but then, there were so many opportunities to do so." What went on at 25,000 feet could not be hidden, good or bad.

As stated, our next flight was again to Munich. And again, the center of the town would be the MPI. We used to joke and say the target was Schultz's Tavern on the corner of Main and Heiney.

Coverage again was ten-tenths, so bombing was PFF. Bombardiers would say they could put a bomb in a pickle barrel using that equipment. Maybe that was true for the first bomb, but I wouldn't want to be within 2 miles of that point on the ground. All other bombs were toggled out over an expanse the size of our wing, and traveling at our high rate of speed, bombs were dropped from 28,000 feet into the undercast below. Flak was as intense as ever. Some of Goering's yellow-nosed fighters hammered us, too, but not in the flak areas.

The Eagle Hunter International reported that, when captured, Goering would possess thousands of morphine pills, would be wearing rouge on his cheeks and have painted toenails. Goering himself was a meddlesome fellow who tried to spread himself too thin. He wanted his name and fame everywhere he could put it. He had an army group named after him and even an element in the Navy. He was the leader of the most powerful air force in the world. An air force that had plenty of money and a production line that was set up even before Hitler was in power. His pilots had a lot of fighting experience before they entered World War II, experience that was gained in the war in Spain. Hitler loved mass fly-bys and used them to intimidate his potential foes. They, along with his screaming Stuka dive-bombers, produced the fear and intimidation he wanted. To produce the Stuka, the production of heavy bombers was cut back. A huge mistake. When Hitler invaded Russia he didn't have the heavy bombers needed to take out the Russian armament factories. Production of the Stuka was discontinued in July 1943. Even though the German Air Force destroyed over 1,000 planes on the first day of the invasion, its weakness contributed greatly to Germany's failed invasion.

Goering's fighters were in rare form this day. They were attacking from the side and from the rear. They were diving from above, firing as they came down on the rear bombers, then coming up from below and hitting us up in front with their 20-mm cannon fire.

Our individual plane was picked by one of the Germany fighters as his primary target. I was doing the flying at the time, and though I never did get a look at who was firing at us, I could see his 20-mm shells exploding just in front of our nose, big bursts of red, spaced like stitching, in front of our plane. With the first burst of red I instinctively pulled up the nose of our ship and cut back on the power. The plane was in an attitude of like mushing along, and the other bombers were pulling ahead of us. Not a good situation, but our skins were saved, just through instinct.

As we mushed along, I could picture the fighter below us in the same attitude, also mushing in the same manner, but unable to slow enough to get his shells into our ship. Dave and Doc were having catfits. Each shook my hand after the flight. As I mentioned earlier, when

Lieutenant James asked, "Do you remember when you saved our bacon?" I was unsure about which mission he was referring to. Well, it was this particular attack. He confirmed it in April of 2000 when we went down to see the very impressive Mighty 8th Air Force Heritage Museum in Savannah, Georgia. Doris and I visited with him and his wife Evelyn on the return trip.

We took a lot of holes in the Sneakin' Deacon. A lot of planes went home, on their own, or under fighter escort, with engines out or burning. Many were knocked out of formation and we never knew what became of them. Two Forts ditched in the sea. Most of the planes that made it back were shooting flares. Lots of dead and wounded. It had been a nine-hour, 20-minute trip. Seven hours of that time on oxygen, at minus 35. Grapevine reported that Mike from Dyersburg was down. Now 19 out of 27. Not one crew had finished its missions yet.

When Americans first came over here, a lot of them gave the English the opinion that all of us were rich and spoiled, that we were over there to win a war that they couldn't. That's how the "overpaid, oversexed and over here" started. As we got our feet wet in the war the attitude began to change, on both sides. The British began to refer to us as "their boys" and "their planes," and our people became less cocky and more understanding.

Shortly after the 8th Air Force arrived in England, General Eaker was attending a ball and was asked to speak. His reply was brief: "We won't do much talking until we've done more fighting. We hope that when we leave, you will be glad that we came. Thank you." It was beginning to look like they'd be glad we came.

There were also branches of our own service that

thought the Air Force pampered its men. With those silver wings, extra pay for flying, and usually better living conditions, it was easy to see why. Except for rules and regulations, our lives were pretty much as they had been as civilians. We got out of bed, went to work, did our job and came back home. Not much like fighting on the ground. Food, and living conditions, were both better than combat troops on the ground received.

But those incentives were not handed out freely, they were meant to entice a certain class of men to volunteer. All flyers in the Air Force were volunteers. Their average age was 19. While living conditions were generally better for these young men, fighting conditions were usually worse. There were several more ways to die in the air than on the ground.

The 43,700 plus deaths in the 8th Air Force covered all of those ways. The 1,741 airmen killed in action in Vietnam and the 20 in the Persian Gulf War covered fewer ways. They weren't having 67 men killed for every 1,000 tons of bombs dropped. When dropping a ton of bombs a minute, as we were at the end of World War II, it didn't take long. Although most KIAs and MIAs occurred early in the war, more bombs were dropped near the end of the war.

Once when we had had several days off in a row, I was to be presented the Distinguished Flying Cross by Colonel Smith. I had seen the notice posted, but didn't think there would be a formation for the presentation. Doc Watson and I were walking past the formation as it was being formed. Doc asked, "Hey, aren't you supposed to get your medal today?" At the time I was wearing a shirt and no blouse. Doc was wearing his blouse, so I borrowed it. I now have a picture in an album at home of a 6-foot-7 colonel pinning a medal on a 5-foot-10 pilot wearing a blouse with sleeves 4 inches too short, and sporting bombardier's wings.

On July 17, 1944, we prepared for our 30ᵗʰ mission, 31ˢᵗ for James, Shay and Brown. Brown was still stable enough to get the job done. He was just quiet and appeared to be in a daze all of the time.

We arrived at the plane after briefing, went through our checklists, then sat in the plane and waited for the flare. Red, the mission is scrubbed; green, start your engines. Sometimes the wait could be an hour or more. Today it was only about 20 minutes. We got a green flare, started our engines, and waited for the plane that we would follow to pass our hardstand.

We took off without incident and assembled with no problems, but not without worry. Even in good weather we worried about assembling. Records showed that 5 percent of all planes lost were lost during assembly, over 300 in all.

We were to bomb a railroad bridge at San Quenton, France; the weather would be CAVU. The flak was as bad as ever, just seemed to get worse each time. As our boys on the ground took more and more territory away from the Germans, the Germans drew back their antiaircraft guns into more compact and intense firing patterns. On that bomb run, it was very intense. Planes were losing engines, and controls and cables were being shot away. The ships dropped their bombs, then fell out of formation with their problems.

Our ship received a lot of holes, some in the self-sealing gas tanks, and the catwalk in the bomb bay was smashed. A large piece of flak came up in back of my seat and continued through the roof of the plane. We passed over Paris on the way back and they shot the hell out of us again. Colonel Nuttall got shot up real bad, lost engines and came close to ditching. When we got back, many killed and wounded were aboard the planes. Our ship was full of holes. We didn't bother to count them, but there had to be more than 50.

A 6-foot 7-inch colonel honors a 5-foot 10-inch lieutenant. Harold Rochette receives his Distinguished Flying Cross medal.

Chapter Eighteen

The Last Mission and on to Sebring

Of the four squadrons in the 384th Bomb Group, our squadron, the 544th, still seems to take more punishment than any of the others. It was that way before we got here and it seems to be that way now.

Our Sneakin' Deacon has flown over 30 missions; other planes had been shot down on their first. The luck of the lottery. One ship, Nine-O-Nine, survived over 100 missions. One tail-gunner, flying out of Italy, finished all of his missions and never fired a gun. Olin Penny, our first tail-gunner, was shot out on his second mission. All the luck of the lottery. If you let it bother you, you could end up like Brown, our radio operator, or worse. You knew it could happen, but you convinced yourself that it would happen to the other guy, not you.

My next mission is all that I need to finish my tour. Preparing for it is much harder than preparing for any of the others. Seems as though so many men get shot down on the last one. Not a fact, it just seems so. Again I was offered the opportunity to take over a crew and fly as first pilot. Again I refused, although this time for a different reason.

Bob James had finished his missions. He had started one mission earlier than I, as a copilot. I would be flying with another crew that, to me, was unknown and untested. I thought it better that their own pilot, who knew the crew's strengths and weaknesses, be in charge and I could add my two-cents worth where needed.

After briefing I drew my parachute, harness, Mae West and escape kit. After a mission we always turned them back in. Since this was my last mission, I could keep the escape compasses, but not the maps or the money that were in the escape kit.

The mission was a factory in Peennemunde, Germany, that made robot bombs. The weather was CAVU at the target but ten-tenths en route. Our IP was to be out in the water, the first time that had happened for us. It was a 9½-hour mission with about seven hours on oxygen. About 20 Me-109s and FW-190s hit us. We had been told that some 190s were equipped with tubes under the wings that could fire a 250-pound shell with a 21-pound warhead. They could sit out there at 1,200 yards, out of range of our guns, and fire their heavy shells into our formation. The Germans produced a total of over 20,000 FW-190s in World War II, in addition to tens of thousands of other fighters, including jet and rocket planes.

The flak that day was again heavy and accurate. I saw, for the first time, flak shells before they exploded. They seemed to come up, sit there for a fraction of a second, then explode, or else they fell from the peak of their flight and then exploded. They had to be close, and right at my level, for me to see that. I also had to be looking at just the right spot when the shell arrived

The German fighters hit us at the end of our bomb run and knocked a couple of our bombers out of the formation. They were hit badly, and as soon as they drifted far enough from the protection of our guns the fighters jumped on them like a school of sharks and shot them down. Flak damage to our plane was relatively light, only about 15 holes, and no damage to the engines.

When we landed at Grafton-Underwood, James was waiting to greet me. We shook hands and had a big laugh for ourselves, the first one since we had arrived here that could really be called a belly laugh. We hung around for a week or more before being sent back to the States. During this time I had the job of censoring the mail that was being sent back to the States. There wasn't much to cut out. Most of the danger was in risqué writings that some of the men were sending to their wives or girlfriends. They were hot enough to set fire to the plane that they were being carried on.

One in our group had an embarrassing experience during that layover. He was at a social gathering, and during a discussion, he stated that his Sunday was never complete until he had his "funnies," meaning the funny papers, comics. A couple of ladies giggled and everything went quiet. Later, in a pub, he found out that in England "funnies" were a lady's privates.

Dave finished his missions on the same day that I did, but with a different crew. The four of us, Dave, Bob, Doc and I, had all finished our missions and would be returning to the States. But before I left, Colonel Smith presented me with a special letter thanking me for my

152 O 8th Air Force Lottery

bravery, dedication and for setting such a fine example. I also received the Air Medal, with three oak leaf clusters, to go with my Distinguished Flying Cross.

Scotland was my first stop on the way home. I spent a day there and then boarded a C-54 for an uneventful flight to New York City. The first thing I did upon landing was to drink all of the milk I could hold. After clearing customs we boarded a bus that took us to a hotel. The bus stopped for a stoplight and a gang of youths spotted us and yelled, "Why are you over here when the war is over there?" If we weren't so happy to be home we would have gotten off and "explained." When I got settled in a hotel room I called Doris and she came down from Connecticut to meet me. We spent a few days in the city before heading for home. Our room at a nice hotel cost $5.00 a night.

After a short time visiting family and friends, my wife and I were sent down to Atlantic City, New Jersey, for R&R (Rest and Recuperation). But, there would be none there. A hurricane had wiped out parts of it. There was no electricity so they put us on a train and sent us down to Miami Beach for a five-day stay. We then returned home, where I awaited my next assignment.

I was home a few days when I received orders to report to Lockborne Army Air Force Base, just outside of Columbus, Ohio, where pilots were trained to be instructors. There we learned the fine points and polish needed to get what we had learned in the ETO across to new Flying Fortress crews. We had a lot of classroom work along with flying every day. During the periods of flying my instructor, a Captain Green, put me through all the trials that James and I had gone through overseas, and then some. Emergency procedures such as pulling two engines, at the same time, on one side of the plane. And that when the plane was in an awkward position, such as when turning to the approach from the base leg when landing.

My stay there was about six weeks. I lived on the base. It was a permanent base, so it had a nice Officer's Club and mess hall. I had a chance to do something that I had not done in a long while—see some football games. Ohio State University was just outside Columbus, and they had a good team that played other leading teams in the country. When I finished instructor training, I went home and waited for the Army Air Force's next pleasure.

As luck would have it, that assignment was as an instructor pilot at a B-17 field in Sebring, Florida. To get there, I purchased a used 1935 Dodge from a man in Meriden, Connecticut. Doris, our son and I set out to drive down. It didn't take long to find out that the car was not in very good shape. By the time we got to Sebring we had used 75 gallons of gas and 54 quarts of oil! Most of the oil was crankcase oil picked up at filling stations. No need to say why.

Rents were hard to come by in Sebring. Our first place was one of a string of chicken coops that a fellow had converted into small apartments. It was comfortable, but we were there only a short while. About that time I had to leave Doris and Buddy in Sebring and go off to Lubbock, Texas, to Instrument Flying Instructor's School. The night I was to leave, Doris prepared a home-cooked dinner with a steak from a small, local market. It must have been native beef that had not been properly aged, because it made me very sick. I spent the entire flight to

Lubbock sitting on the floor of the B-17's radio room. Luckily I was only a passenger on that flight.

My stay in Lubbock lasted six weeks and the entire time was spent in either a Link Trainer or flying the AT-6 on instruments. For my efforts I earned the coveted White Card and qualified as an Instrument Flying Instructor.

After another short stay in Sebring I was sent on another trip. This time to fly a B-17 to Deming, New Mexico, to participate in a bombing demonstration for some Washington brass. Two other B-17s accompanied me. A demonstration was set up for some senators, congressmen and high-ranking service officials. A dummy town was set up in the desert, along with a dummy battleship, bridge, factory buildings and a convoy of ships. Our three B-17s were to fly in formation and bomb the dummy town. A Navy plane would demonstrate skip bombing on the dummy battleship. B-25s would hit the bridge and other types of planes would bomb the factory and strafe the convoy. All this would be viewed by the dignitaries from a bleacher that had been set up a safe distance away.

After we arrived at the base we spent a couple of days lying around, enjoying the pool, and the small town of Deming. Deming looked like the towns we used to see in the cowboy western movies, except some of the streets were paved and the sidewalks on the main street were covered with a wooden awning. The town was dead, so my crew and I spent most of our time in the pool. One of the things that stuck in my mind was how dry the air was in New Mexico. When you came out of the pool and walked the 100 or so feet to the dressing rooms, both you and your bathing suit would be completely dry by the time you got there. Another thing I remember is how hot it was. Before you could sit on one of the metal chairs around the pool you had to first submerge it in the pool for an extended period of time.

After all of the dignitaries arrived we were ready to go. This is where the planners of this demonstration made a colossal mistake. The B-17s were to bomb from the highest altitude, so we were to bomb first. We were only up a few thousand feet and our bombardier, a combat veteran who was used to bombing from miles up, hit our target on the nose. We wiped out the town. We also wiped out all four of the other targets. The other planes dropped their bombs, too, but the show was already over. On the return flight to Sebring, I wondered what it would feel like to step directly from the 120 degrees in New Mexico into the 40 degrees below zero of the skies of Germany.

During the last two trips, Doris and Buddy remained in Sebring. Doris stayed busy looking for a better place to live and finally found one, a house that we could rent in a nice neighborhood. But, in order to get the rent, we were required to buy the furniture and appliances already in the house. It was no big deal, however, because when we left, the new renters had to buy the furniture from us.

Our stay at Sebring was a pleasant one. My job was breaking-in B-17 combat crews. I had most evenings off and we could enjoy them at home or at the Officer's Club. At the base on Saturday night there was dancing to a nice band made up of GIs from the base. A sergeant's singing of "Sentimental Journey" produced calls of repeat every time he sang it.

While at Sebring we became friends with Amos Lunsford and his family. They were about 20 years older than we were, but we got along fine. Their house was on the shore of Lake Jackson, where Amos liked to fish for bass with a long bamboo pole. During the day, when I was flying, I would map out the fishing holes in the lake and we would fish them in the evening. Did OK, too.

Once while stationed in Florida a friend, Bill Jackson, asked me to fly as his copilot on a C-47 flight to a distant state. I mention this only because on the return flight we were flying, on a dark moonless night, over sparsely settled country with very few lights on the ground. With Bill flying the plane on instruments, the lulling drone of the engines, the black ground below with its few lights matching the black sky above with its stars, I had the very soothing feeling of being suspended in space. There was no demarcation line showing where the earth stopped and the sky began. Time had stopped; everything was peaceful and serene. I sat with my head leaning against the window on my right and my gaze focused on all of that emptiness outside. The cabin was dark, except for the fluorescent readings on the instrument panel. Bill must have thought I was asleep. He never spoke for the longest time. I had never had that feeling before and never expect to feel it again. It was probably as close to heaven as I will ever get.

Life was much easier than it had been overseas. I met other pilots who had been in combat and we exchanged stories. One unusual one was told by a Lieutenant Crowe who had been in the 8ᵗʰ. It had to do with two B-17s in his group. One had bounced up and made contact with another plane above it. The top turret guns of the bottom plane pierced the bottom of the other plane and they became bound together in flight. The four engines on the bottom ship were still operating. The top plane, its engines stilled, was a few feet back. An outboard prop of the top plane had bitten into the nacelle of the lower plane and bound them even tighter. The pilot of the bottom plane gunned his engines trying to break free, but it was not to be. They continued their piggyback ride to earth, engines on fire, and crews bailing out. Upon contact with the ground, the top plane slid off the bottom plane, which immediately exploded. The top plane continued on and smashed into, and blew up, a wooden building. All those still on board were killed. It was a very unusual accident, but it would happen at least once again, many years later.

On December 14, 1999, two small planes were landing in Florida, one above the other, and on the same runway. A wheel of the top plane pierced the windshield of the bottom plane and became captive. They landed safely in that position, with no one being injured.

After Lieutenant Crowe had finished his strange tale another in the group added his. Again it was the story of a B-17. The plane had received a direct hit of flak between the waist door and the tail. The blast blew the entire tail section clear of the plane with the stunned tail gunner still in it. The plane went into a direct dive to earth and the blown-off tail section started its flight to earth on its own. Its free fall was slowed down by its own airfoil until it landed in a deep bank of snow. The tail gunner was the only survivor of that bizarre happening. The tail section had "flown" down from 24,000 feet.

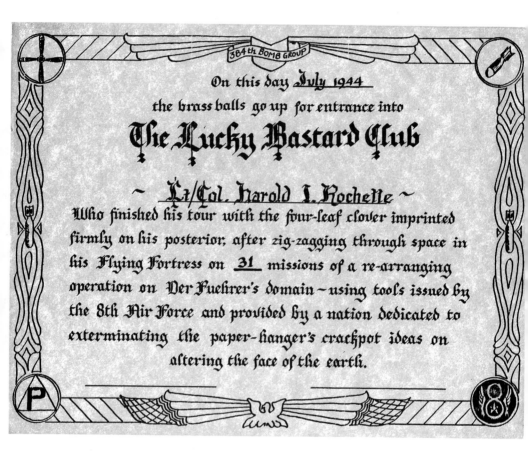

On this day _July 1944_
the brass balls go up for entrance into

The Lucky Bastard Club

~ _Lt/Col. Harold L. Rochette_ ~

Who finished his tour with the four-leaf clover imprinted firmly on his posterior, after zig-zagging through space in his Flying Fortress on _31_ missions of a re-arranging operation on Der Fuehrer's domain ~ using tools issued by the 8th Air Force and provided by a nation dedicated to exterminating the paper-hanger's crackpot ideas on altering the face of the earth.

Harold Rochette's "diploma" finally caught up with him at a 384th Bomb Group reunion after the war.

While comparing dates and missions, we found that my 31 missions in 66 days eclipsed, by far, any of the others' times. Most of them had never heard of pills to stay awake. We must have been in different time frames.

In the group there was controversy about the 8th's dropping of leaflets over towns that were to be bombed. Some thought that the added savings of civilian lives outweighed the extra danger to our flyers. Others debated that view.

Chapter Nineteen

Tampa
and More
Antique Veterans

While at Sebring I made the acquaintance of a Captain Cooper. He was a pilot who had flown with the RAF and transferred over when we entered the war. He had a young collie named Turbo-Supercharger. Every time the dog completed a "mission" on the barracks floor, Cooper recorded it on a chart on the wall. A puddle for one type and a pile for the other. She had quite a few missions.

This same Captain Cooper was involved in a strange accident while we were at Sebring. The Training Command had a procedure where, when flying in formation, one plane flying as a wingman would change places with the other wingman. One plane would swing up and over the tail of the lead plane while the other wingman would slide down and under at the same time.

Cooper was flying as instructor in the plane that was going up and over. In that maneuver it was hard to keep the lead plane in view. Cooper didn't, and sliced the tail off of the lead plane. All ten men in the lead plane were killed. Cooper landed safely. That maneuver was discontinued. It had no use in combat, anyway. Two planes would not exchange positions. One might, to fill in the spot of a plane that had been shot down, but not two. If need be, that one plane would swing under and keep all other planes in view.

V-E Day happened while we were at Sebring. We didn't get to participate in a celebration because there wasn't one. The town was too small, and the base, for some reason, didn't organize one. I learned that the last mission my group flew over in Europe was to Pilzen, Czechoslovakia. The target was the Skoda armament plant. Six B-17s were lost. Must be tough. It could have ended a day earlier and saved 600 men.

After that, things slowed considerably at the Sebring base and the Air Force didn't seem to know what to do with us. They sent me to another B-17 base, Avon Park, only about 10 miles away. It was to be only a holding spot, so Doris and Buddy headed back home until we could see what was to happen — the Pacific, or another base. Seemed like they were moving us around just to keep the paper shufflers busy.

I stayed in Florida. McDill Field was my next assignment. McDill was a B-29 base and I had yet to be checked out in a B-29. Nobody was in much of a hurry to do that, so I had a lot of free time on my hands. They put me in charge of the Supply Depot. I still had a lot of time on my hands, so I went over to the Tampa Airport and took the tests for a commercial pilot's license. I passed it and still have the license. Never used it.

While I was Supply Officer I could have had a portable generator truck for free. It was as big as those big trailer trucks and worth a small fortune. I don't know why, but it was assigned to no one. The only problem was to get it off the base. You would have to prove ownership. Now I knew why it was sitting there.

I found a rent at Maritime Apartments in Tampa, and again sent for Doris and Buddy. The place was livable but full of cockroaches, as was most of Florida at that time. We immediately gained a bunch of friends by setting off a couple of gas bombs while we were away for the weekend, chasing the roaches into the other apartments of that six-apartment building.

There was nothing else to do while on base so I learned to play bridge. There were six or eight of us that got to be pretty good players. We taught our wives. So after playing most of the day on base, we went home and played at night. We even had pairs from other bases fly in to play us after word got around.

World War II was winding down. It was to be the most devastating event in history and would claim between 40 and 50 million lives. Almost two billion people in 61 countries participated. The war cost the United States an estimated 341 billion dollars.

Robert Parisi stated that in a proclamation commemorating the end of World War II, 53 years later. He also listed as one of the three key events of the war, "the air raids that forced Germany to surrender." The other two being the Japanese attack on Pearl Harbor and the dropping of the atomic bomb on Hiroshima, Japan.

While at McDill Field we were doing very little

flying. Hardly enough to meet the minimum to collect flight pay. A cross-country once in awhile. A training flight to Cuba, a good place to pick up booze. While there you could enjoy a bottle of Coca-Cola and two ounces of rum for a dime. It wasn't long before those of us with enough points were offered a discharge, if we so elected. I elected.

Japan had surrendered. I had had enough military for awhile so I accepted the offer and returned to civilian life in January of 1947 with the rank of captain.

Shortly after that, on July 20, 1947, our daughter Barbara was born. She would have a normal childhood and schooling, not learning anything about World War II in school and very little from me. She was 50 years old before she learned that I had participated in D-Day on June 6, 1944. She went on through college, with honors, and now holds a job in Denver as the administrator in an office of 31 lawyers. Her job entails the hiring, firing and supervising of over 80 employees, other than the lawyers.

After a couple of years, I decided to become active in the Air Force Reserve. After 23 more years of study and school, attending classes and meetings, laced with periods of active duty, I was again mustered out of the service. This time as a Lieutenant Colonel, in March 1973.

I wasn't interested in joining any military organizations such as the Veterans of Foreign Wars or the American Legion until 1998. At that time a good friend of mine, and at one time a fellow worker at Connecticut Light and Power, asked me to join a military unit that had just formed. It was being called the Antique Veterans and was being formed with a multi-purpose future in mind. It has no by-laws, no dues and no definite rules or

Seated are the crew members who flew a B-17 on a training flight to Havana, Cuba. The man in white was their guide and interpreter.

"Turbo Supercharger," Captain Cooper's collie, performed her own missions on the barracks floor. The captain cleaned them up expertly before recording them.

regulations. Membership at the time of this writing is more than 200. Weekly meetings are attended by an average of 45 members, more than the monthly attendance at meetings of all other military units in our town combined. Most of our members are veterans of World War II, many with combat experience. Some are decorated and some have been decorated several times. The organization is open to any veteran of any war. Our mission is "To promote patriotism, love of country and respect for the flag." All expenses are paid by the membership, with no outside support at this time.

Storytelling at meetings takes up a great part of our time, but business having to do with our named functions takes precedence. The functions are as follows:

- Address school classes on military holidays
- Address civic groups as requested
- Furnish honor guard, firing squad, bugler and flags for military funerals
- March in military parades, or as requested
- Visit military hospitals
- Appear at social functions, building dedications, and at presentations on national holidays

One function that we're particularly proud of is our system for collecting the tabs from the tops of soda, beer, cat-food and dog-food cans. Our members gather these pull tabs from their friends, relatives, and other organizations to which they belong. They pick up the cans and tabs along the road, at sporting events, bingo games, picnic grounds, and anywhere people gather. Church and senior-citizen groups save them for us. The tabs are then turned over to the Ronald McDonald House. The money from the sale of the tabs is used to subsidize the cost of lodging for the families of sick children, sick children that the Ronald McDonald House is taking care of.

I am in charge of this operation for the Antique Veterans, and a year ago we turned in 551 pounds of tabs. Another 410 pounds will be turned in soon. What other function could be more rewarding than helping these unfortunate children have their families with them, in some cases for the last time?

We Antique Veterans have our own uniforms, purchased individually. We wear no rank. Ribbons for awards and decorations may be worn, along with any special badges. We have our own pennant and banner and 17 flags representing military and civilian units.

As a member of the Antique Veterans I have found a group of men who seem to have the same desires and objectives as I do. More than anything else, I think camaraderie holds us together. The stories and experiences that are told open up the group to more of the same. Some like to tell what they have seen and done, others listen and are interested. Over the past two years more have opened up, men who have been quiet for years. It helps to talk to others who have been through the same thing. In some cases a strong stomach helps. Not everyone has one.

One thing the whole group seems to agree on is the lack of knowledge that the younger generations have of what their elders went through to give them what they have today, things that have not been put in history books and probably never will be. Too many of the younger generations just take their good fortune for granted. No thought is given to the price that was paid, hundreds of thousands killed in battle, thousands in Veteran's homes with limbs missing, eyes sightless or bodies mangled. Too many people today do not know what these letters stand for: KIA, MIA, or POW. Too bad, and with veterans dying at the rate of 1,100 per day, almost too late to learn.

One of the Antique Veterans' most important objectives is to make known to the younger generations what it means to live in a society such as ours. Living free does not mean free living, free living such as existed in the 1960s. The free love, drugs and slovenly living all led to the cultural decline that we have today. The one-parent family, the no-marriage family, a president who would probably be elected again, if he could run, in spite of his lies and the impeachment proceedings taken against him. Then there are the drugs.

We are in bad straits when we have juries granting millions to people who spill hot coffee in their laps and then sue the establishment that served them. Billions of dollars have been awarded because of people who have smoked several packs of cigarettes a day for 30 years and then sue the cigarette manufacturers because of their ills.

It's quite a jump from the kind of people who make up our Antique Veterans, and their families, to the people I have written about in preceding paragraphs. After attending well over 100 of our veterans' meetings I have yet to see one person smoke. Compare that to some of our younger crowd today with their drugs, and some of the stuff they smoke. Gratefully, I think that there are still enough of our sensible young people around to outweigh the irresponsible ones.

The Antique Veterans perform throughout Connecticut. Top: At Hubbard Park in Meriden. Bottom: At the Veterans Home in Rocky Hill.

**Antique Veterans, left to right: Dick Egan, Ed Dering,
Hal Rochette, Ken Dow**

Chapter Twenty

Interesting Bits and Pieces

Interesting side issues having to do with my military career have presented themselves in the past few years, some of them being interesting enough to repeat. One took place as Doris and I were changing planes in Detroit. That day I was wearing my favorite black T-shirt with a picture of a B-17 on the left pocket. As we were boarding the second plane, the flight attendant spotted it and said, "You know, my boyfriend flew a B-17 on the 50th Anniversary of D-Day."

I replied, "I flew a B-17 on the original D-Day."

She was quick to respond, "Oh my God, would he love to talk to you! He's a pilot on this airline but he's not on this flight."

She continued the conversation, holding up the passengers, asking questions of both my wife and me. After we broke free, were seated and in flight, she came back, knelt in the aisle, and continued the conversation.

She said to me, "I would put you in first class, but I have only one empty seat, and I know you wouldn't leave your wife back here alone." She continued, "Although we don't serve drinks on so short a flight, I would like to bring you one. What would you have?" My wife ordered a glass of wine and I a dry-gin martini. As she delivered the drinks she cautioned, "If anyone should ask, just say you're my parents." On the tray in front of me, she placed one martini in a glass and another in a bottle on the side. It wasn't long before she was back again, this time with a bottle of wine, wrapped in a towel, for my wife.

As we left the plane, the attendant took us aside, and we chatted until the plane emptied. She hugged us both as we said good-bye. We left at the same time as the pilots. One pilot noticed the picture of the B-17. He said to me, "You must be the famous B-17 pilot we've been hearing so much about." I replied, "A person can get famous pretty fast on this flight."

It wasn't until we got to our destination, our son's home in Wisconsin, that I read the boarding passes. Doris had been sitting in seat B, in row 17.

Exactly 51 weeks later we again made our annual trip out to Wisconsin. Again, we changed planes in Detroit, on this same airline. This time I was wearing my baseball cap with a B-17 on it. I had also added the ribbons for my DFC and Air Medal, always good for making friends and starting conversations.

As we entered the cabin, the pilot was talking to a flight attendant. He spotted my hat and asked, "Is the hat for real or are you just wearing it?"

I replied, "Both, it is for real and I am wearing it."

At this point the flight attendant turned around and, you guessed it, it was the same one who had been so nice to us the year before.

After surprised greetings, I asked, "Does this airline only have one airplane?"

"No," she said, "we have several, only a last minute change put me on this flight."

We chatted with her at our seats for awhile, and as we left the plane, she again presented us with a bottle of wine, stating, "Every time you fly with me you're going to get a bottle of wine." I wanted to ask where I could get a copy of her flying schedule but quickly decided that might be pushing things a little too far.

In looking back it's easy to see how important, and prominent, the number 17 has been in my life. In addition to the B-17 and the PT-17 that I liked so much, there is my social security number that ends in 17 and my officer's serial number, which also ends in 17. The number keeps popping up in places like my bank account, brokerage account and telephone number.

The B-17 is prominently displayed in my home today. Two 1,000-piece jigsaw puzzle scenes hang over the fireplace and a model B-17 sits on the TV. It's displayed in other places, too. I never want to forget how much I owe to this airplane.

A few years back I tried to present some Christmas candy to a few of my friends. It was ordered from Swiss Colony and was to be sent by mail. I designated the sender as the Sneakin' Deacon. The Swiss Colony Company informed me that they would have to refuse the order if I did not name a new sender. I did.

There were 12,731 B-17s built by Boeing, Douglas

and Lockheed. Only four or five of them are flying today. When they made the movie "Memphis Belle," I was told they used only three B-17s and that one of those crashed. I was at the Boeing plant at the time, and they were worried that the one that crashed might be theirs. It wasn't.

Since joining the Antique Veterans and attending their public functions in uniform, I've been asked to speak to other groups. Sometimes I meet people who are familiar with our much-loved plane. One was a fighter pilot who flew P-51s, furnishing fighter protection to our groups. He said, "We sat out there and watched you fly thought that flak. How could you stand it?"

Another told me he watches the History Channel on TV and "it makes me cry when I see those B-17s going down, in that slow spiral, carrying those men to their deaths." While the number killed or missing in action in the 8th Air Force in World War II was almost 12 percent of all U.S. forces that were killed, it must be remembered how small a part of all those forces the 8th really was, and that only 8.7 percent of the 8th were flyers. If you combined all those KIA in the Revolutionary War, the War of 1812, the Mexican War, the Spanish-American War, the Korean War, Desert Storm and a couple of the smaller ones (such as Grenada and Panama), they still would not reach the losses of the 8th. Even the many years of the Vietnam War produced only about 10,000 more dead. The Korean war 10,000 less. World War I also had 10,000 more KIA.

The seven cemeteries in France and Italy that are home to America's war dead contain 32,000 graves. Many of those dead are part of the 8th's 43,742. The average age of the dead in those cemeteries is 22, and 9,386 are buried overlooking the English Channel and Omaha Beach.

As I think back now on the many things that happened in the war it's amazing how many miracles, near misses and unusual things took place. Many of which I would never have known if I had not been doing research for this book.

We all know that Glen Miller disappeared while flying in a small plane over the English Channel, but no one could say how or why. My research turned up a report by an English observer that gives his account of that loss. The observer was a member of the crew on an English bomber returning from a mission. They were flying in formation with other bombers and were still carrying their bomb loads, which had not been dropped due to their not locating the target in the undercast. As they jettisoned their bomb loads into the English Channel he spotted a small plane below in the path of the bombs being dropped. He saw that plane spin into the water. Could that have been Miller's plane? The time frame of the missing plane and the bomb drop are the same.

There are other things, not so serious, that cause me to chuckle to myself when I remember them. Things such as the roster being called while in the cadets. The alphabetical listing of names, called in sequence, to which the cadets responded. In this case it was Berg, Green, and Greenberg.

The complaint of the farmer near Camden, South Carolina, where we flew our first planes, the PT-17 Steerman. His complaint? "The new pilots are bombing my cows with the cranks used to start the plane's engine, and I have the cranks to prove it!" The response of the

Army Air Force was a bulletin, which read, "Cadets will secure cranks more thoroughly before doing loops."

The thoughts that now cross my mind tell me that parts of the war were fun, the PT-17 and the aerobatics, basking in the admiration of an officer's uniform and a pair of silver wings. And the pride shown by my wife and parents.

Then there are the questions. Why didn't I collect any of those 52 payments of $20 from the 52-20 club that I was entitled to? Too proud, or too stubborn?

That German 20-mm shell that came into the plane in back of my seat but didn't explode. If it had, what would have been the result?

If our cities had a few bombs dropped on them, would it have taught the American people anything? Would they more appreciate the sacrifices that their dead countrymen had made? Would they honor Memorial Day and Veterans Day in greater numbers than they do now? Would they attend the parades, that honor veterans, in greater numbers? Or would so many of them still think of those two days as trips to the mall or to the beach? Would the lady in California still complain of the noise that the Marine helicopters, in training, were making "just to harass residents of my affluent neighborhood"?

Then there was the young woman, carrying a small child, that recently asked a captain in an Air Force uniform, "What are you?" Of course this lack of knowledge, in many cases, is not the fault of only the persons involved. In too many cases it is simply a case of not being taught. The younger generations didn't experience the times of World War II, and the history books seem to treat it like it is something to be swept under the rug. The atrocities committed by the Germans and the Japanese must not be mentioned. There are even people in our country who deny that these things ever happened. There were no death marches, no holocaust, no Japanese soldier Pleasure Houses with their thousands of captured women, some of whom were forced to "serve" up to 100 men a day—each!

In making "Saving Private Ryan," director Stephen Spielberg has taken a big step toward showing people the horrors of war. As Howard Cosell would have said, "He told it like it was." Too bad its showing cannot be made mandatory for the American public. So many children are not even allowed to see it. Too bad also that the feelings of the American public on that day, D-Day, cannot be passed on to the young. The anxiety, the fear, the apprehension. The day that the *New York Daily News* replaced its lead stories with "The Lord's Prayer."

The following generations must understand that what they enjoy today came at a price. Our teachings should be directed to the generation now in elementary schools and above. Too many have already been lost in the generations following ours.

John Omicinski wrote a beautiful column on the unsung GIs of World War II. "Let's offer one more snappy salute to the fabulous GI Generation." He says the GI Generation was the key to defeating Germany and Japan, and then containing the evil Soviet Empire. "It was one of a kind. We will not see its match." When we were attacked in 1941, there was virtually no U.S. Army, Navy or Air Force. "The GIs performed miracles. By war's end our armed forces numbered 12 million. Our war workers produced 300,000 aircraft, 72,000 navel vessels and 87,000 tanks. U.S. production was double Germany's and Japan's combined."

He further states, "They had been poorly remembered by the nation, until five years ago, on the anniversary of D-Day. It is possible that we have become hopeless, where knowledge of history is concerned, which is a very dangerous place for any country to be... . The GI Generation will be remembered. There has never been one quite like it. It's hard to imagine that there could ever be again."

Our Antique Veteran's group and our speakers are helping to tell the story. More groups, following our lead, are being formed in other towns and other states. Some have asked to use our name, logo and patch.

With more veterans dying every day, the task of educating our children is being fitted into a very small time frame. With a group such as the Antique Veterans we have men who fought in every branch of the service and they all have stories to tell, stories that the kids should hear.

They should hear Bill Godburn tell of the freed American prisoners of war, men that he cared for on their flight home from Germany. How they were so emaciated that cardboard boxes had to be put over them to keep the sheets from touching them. They should also know of the many killed in training missions before even getting to combat. The SNAFU (Situation Normal All Fouled Up) Operation Tiger, where so many men died from our own fire in a training operation. They were secretly buried and orders were issued to keep it quiet. The British Admiral in charge of that one committed suicide.

In a D-Day training operation 749 servicemen died when a convoy they were in was not properly protected. Two escort ships had been provided to protect against German subs. One of the escort ships had problems and had to return to base leaving 3,500 men protected by one ship. German subs found the convoy and 749 men were wasted, using today's term for killed. How appropriate.

The previously mentioned death march of 6,000 airmen POW's across Germany in the middle of one of its worst winters where more than 1,300 of them died. Events such as those listed above have never reached most of our history books. How will our grandchildren know of the sacrifices of our generation if we do not tell them? Even their teachers don't know of the hardships of World War II, when millions of Americans were in the armed forces.

Revisionists would change history by distorting, or deleting, the facts. Military holidays are barely mentioned in our local paper, if at all. Parades have more participants than viewers. It would seem that the fault must be shared by all: the schools, the teachers, the distorters of history, and the lazy citizens who do not practice their privilege of voting and civic involvement. We should add ourselves to the list for allowing it to happen.

That's one reason why I belong to the Antique Veterans. They are active, they are becoming known and they are making themselves heard. We are getting into schools and civic organizations to tell people what we did, things that are not in the history books. I recently joined the Army Air Force Round Table, a group that does some of the same things the Antique Veterans do.

I try to tell the younger children many interesting

things, but there are also some things that I won't tell them. I won't tell about the kid in aviation cadet training with the problem teeth. He appeared to be about 17 years old. His black hair dropped down over his forehead much like Hitler's. When he put a black comb under his nose and spoke in German-like gibberish, he gave an excellent imitation of the paperhanger. An Army dentist told him that all of his teeth had to come out. He cried like a baby. He was too shook up to give us the reason. After all, having all of his teeth pulled at 17 was enough to make us cry along with him.

There are also things that you tell only to selected groups. Like the uses that servicemen found for condoms, things other than what they were intended for. Riflemen used them to protect the barrels of their guns. Soldiers tied them around their ankles to blouse their trousers. One GI told me that they once used the gas jets in a barracks to fill condoms with gas. They then tied a piece of paper to it, put a match to the paper and let it go. The balloon rose until the flames burned through and ignited the gas. The result was like an aerial bomb. Another use that I have already told you about, to dispose of urine while on a mission. The forerunner to the A-bomb and the H-bomb could be called the P-Bomb. Condoms were also used to store valuables that needed to stay dry.

After I retired from the active Air Force Reserve I kept in touch with only two of my crew, Bob James and Dave Bronstein. James had stayed in the Air Force and Bronstein was called back for the Korean War before he retired. All three of us retired as lieutenant colonels. I talked to Doc Watson once on the phone. True to his word, he never did leave his hometown.

Dave and his Dorothy and I and my Doris got together at one of the 384ᵗʰ reunions. We knew each other, and that was about it. We decided that reunions were for the people who had spent a few years together. We had only been with the group for about three months. We visited them once more at their home in Florida. Dave was kind enough to give up some of his time during Yom Kippur for us. He died a few years later.

Doris and I visited Bob and Evelyn James at their home in Virginia, where, as a hobby, Bob kept bees and sold honey. He marketed the product labeled as "Colonel James Honey." Sales were slow, so he changed the label to "Farmer James Honey" and they took off.

We saw Bob and Evelyn only that one time in the last 55 years, but we had corresponded over those years. We saw them again in April of 2000, when we visited the Mighty 8th Museum in Savannah. The Mighty 8th showed the 384ᵗʰ banner, a monument to the 384ᵗʰ Bomb Group and, best of all, a plaque chiseled in granite listing the name of our plane, the Sneakin' Deacon, and the names of our crew and their positions on the ship. It also stated that all survived. The plaque is placed next to the 384ᵗʰ monument. Bob James had it placed there.

In October 1996, 52 years and three months after my last mission, I again flew in a B-17. Two planes were touring the U.S., a B-17 and a B-24. That group, and my hometown newspaper, the Meriden *Record-Journal*, got together and made a feature story of the flight. Julie Fishman, the journalist, interviewed me and read my journal. She and a photographer joined me on the flight. The next day the story, and pictures, took up half the front page. My claim to fame.

To the best of my knowledge, all events, stories and happenings in this book are true, even though I didn't witness all of them. Some of the information is from government publications. Some names have been changed.

I end this book like I ended my World War II journal: "I HAVE HAD IT."

Reliving old memories. This photo was taken just before the takeoff of Harold Rochette's last flight on a B-17, October 9, 1996. This B-17 is one of the World War II aircraft that the Collings Foundation of Massachusetts exhibits around the country.

Ode to the Bombardier

On a lonely road, on a cold bleak night,
A grizzled old man trudged into sight.
And the people whispered over their beers,
"There goes the last of the bombardiers."

"What is a bombardier?" – No reply.
The men turn silent and the women sigh,
As a death like silence fills the place
With the gaunt, gray ghost of a long lost race.

It's hard to explain, that catch of breath,
As they seemed to sense the approach of death.
Furtive glances from ceiling to floor
Till someone, or something, opened the door.

The bravest of hearts turned cold with fear,
The thing in the door was a bombardier.

His hands were bony and his hair was thin,
his back was curved like an old bent pin.
His eyes were two empty rings of black,
and he vaguely murmured, "Flak, flak, flak."
This ancient relic of the Second World War
crept cross the room and slouched to the bar.

No one spoke, but they watched in the glass,
as the old man showed a worn bombsight pass,
and with hollow tunes from his shrunken chest,
demanded a drink and only the best.

The glass to his lips, they heard him say,
"The bomb bay's open... bombs away!"
With no other word, he sneaked through the door,
and the last Bombadier was seen no more.

—Author Unknown

Robert James had this granite marker placed at the Mighty 8th Air Force Museum in Savannah, Georgia. It was at Savannah that the 8th Air Force was originally formed.

This monument was erected at the airfield of the 384ᵗʰ Bomb Group in England. When the airfield was converted to farmland, the monument was moved to the Mighty 8ᵗʰ Museum in Savannah, Georgia.

Glossary

Ace	Pilot with five or more enemy planes shot down
Buncher Beacon	Gathering place for bombers
CAVU	Ceiling and Visibility Unlimited
Chaff	Strips of aluminum
CO	Commanding Officer
D-Day	First day of invasion
D-Hour	Hour of invasion
ETO	European Theatre of Operations
Flak	Bursts of shells from ground batteries
Focke-Wulf	German manufacturer of FW-190 fighter plane
GI	Government Issue (soldier)
GP	General-purpose bombs for any target
IP	Initial point, i.e. where the bomb run started
KIA	Killed In Action
Mae-West	Inflatable vest similar to today's water wings

ME	Maximum Effort
Me-109	Messerschmitt fighter
MIA	Missing In Action
Milk run	Short, easy run. Comparatively little danger.
MM	Millimeter
MP	Military Police
MPI	Main Point of Impact
PFF	Path Finder
POAE	Point of Aerial Embarkation
POW	Prisoner Of War
PX	Post Exchange
RAF	Royal Air Force
RPM	Revolutions Per Minute
R&R	Rest and Recuperation
SOL	Shit-Outa-Luck
VFW	Veterans of Foreign Wars
Window	Chaff, strips of aluminum

About the Author

On the last day of school in the fourth grade, I was thrown out of school. I had hit the teacher, Miss Hughs, in the head with a rubber ball that we were throwing around. It was an accident but it didn't matter, I was out. I couldn't go home, so I spent the rest of that rainy afternoon hiding in an empty chicken coop until the class got out. The rest of my schooling was normal, right through high school.

In high school I participated in football, basketball and track. Never outstanding, but good enough to play. I also played some semi-pro football and basketball after high school. In my sophomore year, I met Doris Stange. We went together until we were married in 1941.

As a kid, my first job was weeding onions on a truck farm for ten cents an hour. I progressed to 35 cents an hour on my next job as a gardener, and then did a little better as a hauler in the tobacco fields. Other jobs that I held in my youth included soda jerk, door-to-door salesman, store clerk, painter's helper, and laborer. As a laborer, I once pushed wheelbarrows full of cement for 14 hours, in a boiling sun, and then took Doris to her Senior Ball that night.

My next job was at Pratt & Whitney, where I was paid a very good wage, and a bonus that sometimes reached well over 100 percent. Pratt & Whitney was a defense factory, but when the United States entered World War II, I decided I wanted to try flying the engines I'd been working on. To accomplish that, I began studying for the examination that would make me an Aviation Cadet. This book covers what happened from then to my time in the active reserve.

While I was in the active reserve, I worked for the Connecticut Light and Power Company. Because I wanted to work outside, I took a job as a lineman. When the company needed a head instructor for its new Hot Line Stick Training Program, I was selected because of my background as an instructor in the Air Force. I was given a free hand to set up the school, the tests, and the training area for training more than 600 lineman. Four instructors were assigned to work for me, and I was handed the added assignments as chairman of the newly organized Tool and Equipment Committee and the drafting of Work Practices and Procedures for the Transmission and Distribution Departments.

Hot-stick work was entirely new to our whole system. We had used hot sticks right along to pull cutout boxes and switches, but not on the major scale being contemplated.

The author, above left, teaching at the Northeast Utilities Training School in 1956. Here he shows trainees the hot-stick method, at low level, for splicing a live conductor. Normally, the men would work at the top of a pole, as shown in the photo below.

The company sent me out to Centralia, Missouri, where the A.B. Chance Company manufactures its tools. I saw how the hot sticks were made and used and then went through a two-week training course. At that time the sticks were all wood, in some cases with strips laminated and the grain reversed for strength. They were kiln dried to remove moisture and to cut down on conductivity, then coated with plastic to hold them in that condition. Working with those tools was much like working with your hands, except you were 6 to 10 feet away from the work. The sticks ranged in diameter from 1½ inches to 4 inches and from 3 feet to 14 feet in length. We could do any job with those tools that we could do with our hands, including complete pole changeovers. The sticks were meant to be used on all voltages above rubber-glove range (5,000 volts).

While working as a hot-line instructor, I traveled to upstate New York to train with a crew handling 345,000-volt lines, bare-handed. It was done from a bucket truck with a grid in the basket and a cage in back and over it. To do it, you clipped in and were part of the circuit. If you were to spit from the bucket, you would get a flash back of electricity to your lip. If you were to roll a cigarette, the tobacco would float in midair, as it would in the weightlessness of outer space. Otherwise, you were like a bird sitting on a wire. I'm sure I was the first and probably the only person in Connecticut to bare-hand 345,000 volts. Bare-handing is a common everyday occurrence out there now.

I worked for Connecticut Light and Power, and then Northeast Utilities when they merged, for 35 years. I retired in April 1984, with 35 years of service and 3½ workdays missed due to sickness or injury.

Acknowledgments

As you can see, I'm not really a writer. A story-teller, maybe. Many hours were put into research to find materials other than my own experiences to make this book more interesting reading. Sorting, assembling, and phrasing that information would have been much harder without the help of my wife, Doris. I must also thank her for her help in spelling and punctuation, as I was poor at both in school and she was always on the high-honor roll, English included.

For allowing me to use their invaluable personal and observed stories in this book, I thank fellow Antique Veterans Richard Egan, Robert Coffey, Edward Dering, Kenneth Dow, William Godburn, Frank Lamphier, Raymond Weckworth, Joseph Borriello, Neville Wolf, Joseph Wysocki, Henry Muszynski, Raymond Petrosky, Chip Clark, and all those other dedicated Antique Veterans.

Tom Brokaw, with his two books, *The Greatest Generation* and *The Greatest Generation Speaks*, prodded me into writing this book. For that I thank him. He reminded Americans how great the World War II generation has been, calling us "the greatest generation that ever lived." He further stated that we were dying at the rate of 1,100 a day and that we must tell our kids about our trials and experiences before our time runs out. That's what I'm doing—telling our children and grandchildren, mine and yours, the things that are not in U.S. history books. Things that our politicians, and the business world in many instances, would like us to forget.

Events depicted in this book that are not personal experiences were told to me by the people who experienced or witnessed them—the stories within my story. Some of the names have been changed.

Many thanks are due to that beautiful B-17G, the "Sneakin' Deacon," without whose help this book could never have been written.

On the pages of this book are many of my own personal experiences that took place while I was flying with the 384th Bomb Group in England. Anyone who would like an excellent history of this Bomb Group should obtain a copy of the publication "as briefed" by Walter E. Owens.

My thanks for those facts and figures that came from publications where the authors were unknown. Many, however, came from Army Air Force or other government publications.

It would be impossible to close these acknowledgments without saying how grateful I am to Karyn Krystock for all her help. Her tireless typing, and her invaluable counseling and guidance, could not be more appreciated.

Further Reading

Astor, Gerald. *The Mighty Eighth: The Air War in Europe As Told by the Men Who Fought It (Dell World War II Library)*. New York: Dell Publishing Co., 1998

Bowman, Martin W. *B-17 Flying Fortress*. Crowood Press, 1998

_____. *B-17 Flying Fortress Units of the Eighth Air Force (Combat Aircraft, 18)*. Osprey Publishing Co., 2000

Freeman, Roger A. *The Mighty Eighth: Units, Men and Machines (A History of the U.S. 8th Army Air Force)*. Garden City, New York: Doubleday and Company, Inc., 1970

Hess, William N. *Great American Bombers of WWII: B-17 Flying Fortress*. Osceola, Wisconsin: MBI Publishing Company, 1998

_____. *Hell in the Heavens: Ill-Fated 8th Air Force Bomb Group Missions*. Specialty Press, 2000

Jablonski, Edward. *Flying Fortress: The illustrated Biography of the B-17s and the Men Who Flew Them*. Garden City, New York: Doubleday & Company, Inc., 1965

Johnson, Frederick A., Boyne, Walter J. *B-17 Flying Fortress: The Symbol of Second World War Air Power*. McGraw-Hill Professional Publishing, 2000

McGuire, Melvin W., Hadley, Robert (Introduction). *Bloody Skies: A 15th AAF B-17 Crew: How They Lived and Died*. Yucca Tree Press, 1999

McLaughlin, J. Kemp. *The Mighty Eighth in WWII: A Memoir*. Lexington, Kentucky: University Press of Kentucky, 2000

Novey, Jack. *The Cold Blue Sky: A B-17 Gunner in World War Two*. Howell Press, 1997

O'Neill, Brian D. *Half a Wing, Three Engines and a Prayer*. McGraw-Hill Professional Publishing, 1999

Smith, Truman, Kennedy, Byron L. (Ed.), Weber, Carlton (Introduction). *The Wrong Stuff! The Adventures and Misadventures of an 8th Air Force Aviator*. Southern Heritage Press, 1997

Verlinden, Francois. *Lock on No. 24: Boeing B-17G Flying Fortress*. Verlinden Productions, Inc., 1994

Index

13th wing, 124
384th Bomb Group, 23-28, 51, 59-62, 84, 104, 107, 111, 139, 149, 158, 180, 187, 195
45th wing, 124
544th squadron, 26, 60, 62, 70, 149
544th Squadron, 26
545th squadron, 60
546th squadron, 60
547th squadron, 60
8th Air Force, 10- 17, 19-27, 29-39, 41-58, 60- 64, 66-72, 74-77, 79- 85, 87-95, 97-105, 107- 116, 118-122, 124-132, 134-148, 150-159, 161-169, 171-189, 191-195
8th Air Force News, 31
Ace (Flying), 118, 188
Air Force Reserve, 163, 179
Air Force, U.S., 129
Air Medal, 152, 171
Air Transport Command, 124
airsick, 12
Alabama, Maxwell Field, 10, 18, 20-24, 29, 32
Montgomery, 21, 22
Allies, 79, 85, 97-100
Antique Veterans, 124, 136, 160, 163, 166, 167, 168, 169, 173, 177, 178, 194
Anzio, 137
Arado 234, 113, 114
Army Air Force, 10-17, 19-22, 24-27, 29-39, 41-58, 60-64, 66-72, 74-77, 79, 80-85, 87, 88- 95, 97-105, 107-116, 118-122, 124, 125, 126-132, 134-148, 150-159, 161-169, 171- 189, 191-195
Army Air Force Round Table, 178
AT-10, 37, 40
AT-6, 154
Aviation Cadet Corps, 10, 14
B-17 (Flying Fortress), 9, 10, 19, 25, 38, 40, 43-45, 55, 68, 73, 76, 78, 81, 84, 85, 97, 103, 106, 112, 113, 127, 128, 130, 135, 136, 142, 152-155, 157, 161, 164, 170-172, 180, 183
B-25, 50, 80, 154
B-29, 161

Baer, Heinz, 118
Baldwin, Ivy, Sgt., 27
Barkhorn, Gerhard, Maj., 118
Basic Training School, 28, 32, 33, 34, 37, 40
Bataan Death March, 30
Benzedrine, 86, 87, 101, 109, 129
BF-100s, 58
bikes, 59, 88, 104
Bloody 100th, 103, 124
body-building (for pilots), 21
bombs, 12, 25, 43, 57, 66, 69, 73, 78, 80-84, 92, 94- 97, 103, 104, 106, 116, 117, 119, 120, 124, 125, 127, 133, 134, 138, 139, 142, 146, 151, 154, 155, 162, 174, 179, 185, 188
Bombardier School, 68
bombing missions, 16, 24-27, 44, 51-53, 56, 58, 62, 65-70, 73, 77-81, 83-91, 93, 94, 96, 98, 100-104, 107-109, 112, 113, 116-122, 124, 126-130, 138, 139, 142, 144, 146, 149- 151, 159-161, 164, 165, 174, 177, 179, 180
British, 16, 23, 50, 60, 79, 84, 106, 130, 131, 144, 177
British Lancaster bomber, 60
Bronstein, Dave, 12, 13, 23-25, 59, 60, 68, 73, 77, 105, 110, 111, 127, 132, 134, 143, 151, 179, 180
Brown, Joe E., Sgt., 13, 76, 79, 91, 102, 105, 132, 134, 146, 149
Brussels, Belgium, 40, 116
BT-13 Vultee Vibrator, 32, 33, 37
Buccleuch, Duke of, 25
Bumbartel, 139
Burma Road (obstacle course), 21
buzz bombs, 65, 67
C-47, 16, 156
C-54, 152
cadet, 10, 15, 24, 29, 30, 41, 179
Cadet Killer (obstacle course), 21
Cadet Training Program, 32
cartoons (on envelopes), 29, 36
chaff, 69, 87, 109
Chinese, 63
Colorado, Denver, 163

colorblindness, 14
Colt 45-caliber, 45, 90, 93, 94, 129, 165
Colt, 45-caliber, 79
Connecticut, Hartford, 10, 14
    Meriden, 20, 153, 168, 180
    Middletown, 10
Connecticut Light and Power, 163, 191, 193
Constance, Lake, 139
contrails, 64, 92, 101
copilot, 9, 10, 25, 46, 51, 72, 75, 88, 93, 107,
    120, 150, 156
Cordell Hull Hotel, 42, 43
cross-country flight, 33, 47, 163
Cuba, 27, 163, 164
Czechoslovakia, Pilzen, 161
D-Day (June 6, 1944), 13, 14, 71, 90-96, 99,
    108, 163, 170, 176-178, 188
Distinguished Flying Cross, 145, 148, 152
Doolittle, Jimmy, Lt. Col., 50
Dornier 217, 62
dummy airfield/bombs, 79, 80
Duncan, Asa N., Brig. Gen., 50
Egan, Dick, 125, 126, 169, 194
Eisenhower, Dwight D., Gen., 98, 155
Eleanor Cross, 61, 110
engineer, 15, 55, 134
England, 24, 25, 28, 50, 53, 56, 61, 63, 66, 67,
    70, 76, 88, 98-100, 109, 111, 117, 119, 124,
    128, 136, 144, 151, 187, 195
    Bovington, 24
    Brigstock, 59, 110, 121
    Geddington, 55, 59, 61, 89, 110, 121
    Grafton-Underwood, 24, 28, 51, 60, 93,
        121, 135, 151
    Hanley, 24
    Kettering, 24, 121
    Stone, 24
English Channel, 56, 84, 91, 94, 98, 107, 174
Europe, 7, 31, 84, 161
European Theater of Operations (ETO), 9,
    11, 41, 47, 152, 188
first mission, 51, 52, 53, 65, 66, 69, 120
Fishman, Julie, 180
Florida, Avon Park, 161
    McDill Field, 161, 162

Miami Beach, 152
    Sebring, 149, 153, 154, 155, 156, 160, 161
    Tampa, 160, 161, 162
Flying Fortress, See B-17
Focke-Wulf 90 (FW-90), 58
Focke-Wulf factory, 53, 62, 81, 114, 188
Fort Devens, Massachusetts, 31
France, Blainsville, 70
    Caen, 96
    Calais, 65, 120, 133
    Cande, 100
    Cherbourg, 94
    Dreux, 109
    Dunkirk, 70
    Lyon, 117
    Neufchatel, 89, 128
    Rouen, 51
    San Quenton, 146
    Sens, 126
French, 67, 111, 134
Gable, Clark, 86
Georgia, Savannah, 51, 144, 180, 186, 187
German Aces, 118
Germans, 11, 58, 62, 69, 76, 79, 80, 82, 84, 96-
    100, 103, 113-115, 118, 121, 122, 125, 126,
    130, 141, 146, 150, 176
Germany, 50, 53, 78, 80, 85, 86, 99, 108, 119,
    123, 138-143, 150, 155, 162, 176-178
    Berlin, 68, 69, 125, 126
    Bremen, 123
    Cologne, 80
    Halberstadte, 86
    Hamburg, 119
    Leipzig, 115
    Mannheim, 73
    Munich, 138, 139, 140, 142
    Nuremberg, 106
    Peenemunde, 150
    Setten, 53
Gestapo, 140
GI Generation, 176, 177
Godburn, Bill, 177, 194
Goering, Herman, 85, 142, 143
Goldwater, Barry, Sen., 86, 128
Great Lakes, 40, 47

Great War, The, 26
Green, Capt., 152, 174
Greenland, 11, 12
gunner, 66, 73, 75, 79, 82, 86, 87, 103, 107,
    127, 128, 129, 134, 157
Hackl, Anton, 118
Hafner, Anton, 118
Halbeib, Lt., 109
Hanson, Lt., 123
Hiroshima, Japan, 162
Hitler, 31, 68, 99, 100, 140, 142, 143, 179
Iceland, 5, 11, 14, 17, 18, 23
Illinois: Chanute Field, 47
    Chicago, 135
    George Field, 37, 40
Instrument Flying Instructor School, 153-
    154
Ireland, Nuttes Corner, 23, 24
Italy, 85, 103, 124, 136, 149, 173
Jackson, Bill, 156
James, Evelyn, 43, 46, 56, 144, 180
James, Robert, Lt., 9-11, 14-16, 18, 24, 43, 45,
    46, 52-56, 67, 69, 70, 73, 75, 79, 82, 85, 88,
    89, 91, 93, 95, 101, 102, 105, 107, 109, 112,
    119, 120, 127, 132, 144, 146, 150-152, 179,
    180, 186
Japanese, 30, 31, 43, 114, 137, 162, 176
Johnson, Bob, 43, 46, 48, 51, 88, 90
JU-88, 124
June 6, 1944 (see D-Day), 13, 96, 163
Junkers-88, 62
Kennedy, Joe, 97, 113
Kennedy, John F., Pres., 97
Kesselring, Albert, Field Marshall, 85
Kew, John, SSgt., 67
Kittel, Otto, 118
Labrador, 9, 10, 11, 48
    Goose Bay, 10, 11, 12, 23, 48
Landry, Tom, 86, 128
Legion of Merit, 104
Lipfert, Hauptmann Helmut, 118
Luftwaffe, 85
Lunsford, Amos, 156
Mae West, (life vest), 16, 54, 130, 150
Marines, U.S., 141

McCarthy, Joe, Sen., 128
McGovern, George, Sen., 128
Me-163, 114
Me-262, 113
Me-328, 130, 131
Meriden Record-Journal, 180
Messerschmitt 109 (Me-109), 57, 62, 82, 189
    Me-110, 62
    Me-210, 62
Mighty 8th Air Force Heritage Museum, 144
Miller, Glen, 174
Mississippi River, 44
Mistel, 130
Mitchell, Billy, Gen., 129
navigator, 12, 68, 134
Navy, U. S., 63, 93, 129, 137, 140-142, 154,
    176
New Hampshire, Grenier Field, 10, 48
New Jersey, Atlantic City, 152
New Mexico, Deming, 154
New York, Bronx, 29, 32, 79
    New York City, 22, 79, 152
Nikitich, Ivan, Maj., 118
Nine-O-Nine, 149
no-ball targets, 65, 97, 128
Normandy, 100
North Dakota Sate University, 63
North Sea, 97
Nuttall, Lt. Col., 26, 93, 147
observation balloon, 27
obstacle courses, 21
Ohio, Columbus, 152, 153
    Lockborne Army Air Force Base, 152
Omaha Beach, 98, 99, 174
Omicinski, John, 176
Operation Tiger, 177
Pacific (war), 16, 31, 137, 161
parachutes, 12, 51, 53, 54
Parisi, Robert, 162
Pathfinder B-17s, 67
Patton, George S., Gen., 79
Pearl Harbor, 41, 43, 162
Penny, Olin, Sgt., 65, 66, 67, 149
Phase Five, 71
Phase Training, 41

pilotless planes, 63
Point of Aerial Embarkation (POAE), 9, 189
Poland, Pozen, 81
pork chops and Brussels sprouts, 89
Pratt & Whitney, 20, 32, 191
Pre-Flight School, 29
Primary Training School, 28, 32, 34, 35, 37
Prussia, 140
PT-17 Steerman, 28, 32, 37, 174
Pyle, Ernie, 62
Quonset hut, 24
radio operator, 13, 91, 102, 149
Rall, Gunther, 118
Red Cross, 67
Rochette, Barbara (daughter), 163
    Doris (wife), 21, 22, 33, 42, 43, 46, 68,
        120, 144, 152, 153, 155, 161, 162, 170,
        171, 180, 190, 191, 194
    Harold (Buddy), 22, 42, 68, 72, 126, 153,
        155, 161, 162
    Rose (daughter-in-law), 20, 22, 140, 141
Rommel, Erwin, Gen., 99, 100
Rooney, Andy, 108, 142
Rose Garden, 20
Royal Air Force, 50, 51, 97, 103, 160, 189
Rudorffer, Erich, 118
Russia, Pltava, 124
Russian, 118, 124, 126, 143
Russian Aces, 118
salute, 32, 176
Sarver, Sgt., 82, 105, 132, 134
Schweinfurt raid, 27
Scotland, Stornway, 23, 152
Shay, James, Sgt., 15, 55, 105, 132, 134, 146
silver wings, 41, 145, 175
Skoda, 161
Slovak, Pvt., 137
Smith, Dale O., Col., 26, 84, 88, 145, 151
solo flight, 29, 30
SOS, 13, 14, 16
South Carolina, Camden, 28- 32, 35, 37, 174
    Shaw Field, 31, 32, 37, 40
    Sumpter, 31, 32
Southern Aviation School, 28
Speer, Albert, 85

Spitfires, 51
St. Mihiel offensive, 26
Stewart, Jimmy, 86, 128
Stuka, 143
Sturmstaffel One, 114, 115
Summerville, Lt., 111
targets, 16, 45, 53, 56, 57, 65-68, 80-82, 86, 87,
    89, 90, 94-98, 106, 107, 109, 111-113, 117,
    119, 120, 123, 126, 128, 130, 131, 133, 138,
    142, 143, 150, 155, 161, 174, 188
Tennessee, Dyersburg, 40-44, 46-48, 51, 66,
    70, 94, 108, 109, 123, 139, 141, 144
    Memphis, 46, 62, 63, 173
    Nashville, 20
Texas, Lubbock, 153, 154
Texas A& M, 63
Titanic, 12
Tokyo, 50
Truman, Harry, Pres., 129
Uncle Sam (United States), 88, 89
United States, 26, 88, 89, 93, 100, 109, 111,
    113, 114, 126, 129, 137, 140, 141, 162, 173,
    176, 177, 180, 191, 195
Utah, Ogden, 10, 48
V-1 and V-2 rockets, 97, 128
V-E Day, 161
Virginia, 43, 56, 180
Wash, The, 67, 127
Watson, Gaven "Doc", 13, 16, 24, 25, 52, 57,
    73, 77, 83, 105, 127, 132, 143, 145, 151, 179
West Point, 21, 24, 26
West Wall, 65, 90
White Cliffs of Dover, 70, 90
Whitley Hotel, 22
Whole nine yards, The (expression), 16, 53
windmilling, 47, 76, 120, 134, 135
wingman, 76, 120, 160
Wisconsin, 171
World War I, 25, 26, 31, 43, 70, 81, 129, 136,
    137, 141, 142, 145, 150, 162, 163, 165, 173,
    175, 176, 178, 181, 183, 191
World War II, 31, 43, 81, 129, 136, 137, 141,
    142, 145, 150, 162, 163, 165, 173, 175, 176,
    178, 181, 183, 191